George Bidwell

True History of the so-called £1,000,000 Forgery, the Bank duped

How the impregnable Bank of England showered its Bags of Gold on George Bidwell

George Bidwell

True History of the so-called £1,000,000 Forgery, the Bank duped

How the impregnable Bank of England showered its Bags of Gold on George Bidwell

ISBN/EAN: 9783337119645

Printed in Europe, USA, Canada, Australia, Japan

Cover: Foto ©ninafisch / pixelio.de

More available books at **www.hansebooks.com**

TRUE HISTORY

OF THE SO-CALLED

£1,000,000

FORGERY

THE BANK DUPED

HOW THE IMPREGNABLE

BANK ᐧ OF ᐧ ENGLAND

Showered Its

BAGS OF GOLD

ON

GEORGE BIDWELL

AN

American and a Stranger

50 Cents

The Bidwell Publishing Co

HARTFORD, CONN.

TESTIMONIALS AS TO ITS INTEREST.

John C. New, ex-U. S. Treasurer,

Introducing Mr. Bidwell to General McCauley at the Gilsey House, New York, said to the latter, "I have read 'Forging His Chains' through (this during a hot political campaign), my wife has read it, my children have read it, and we all regard it as a book of surpassing interest."

Clarence A. Seward, Esq.,

of the great law firm of Seward, DaCosta & Co., New York: "I have read 'Forging His Chains' with great interest, and, guided by my own experience and knowledge [as attorney for the Bank of England in the Bidwell forgery case], I am convinced of the truthfulness of Mr. Bidwell's narrative."

Robert G. Ingersoll.

"I have read 'Forging His Chains' with much interest, and believe it will do a great deal of good."

Ex-Judge Reynolds

writes: "'Forging His Chains' is a story of absorbing, sometimes dramatic, interest," etc.

The Worcester Spy.

"'Forging His Chains' is a book that has been compared with Dumas's famous 'Monte Christo.' The extraordinary character of its adventures, indeed, would render it dramatic and powerful as fiction; as human truth, it is simply overwhelming. No one can read this book unmoved. From every conceivable standpoint, psychological, sociological, and literary, it is a marvel."

Hartford Daily Times.

"This autobiography is a story of thrilling interest."

New York Mail and Express.

"His book is one of the most interesting that has ever been published."

Boston Herald.

"A very remarkable book of thrilling interest."

New York World.

"'Forging His Chains' is a powerful autobiography."

Boston Globe.

"Mr. Bidwell gives the story of a career which can probably not be equaled."

New York Herald.

"This is a remarkable book."

Inter-Ocean, Chicago.

"'Forging His Chains' is a remarkable narrative, told by the principal actor in some of the most stupendous forgeries of the century."

New York Tribune.

"Mr. GEORGE BIDWELL: *Dear Sir,*—A review of your interesting book is in type, and will be used soon.   Yours truly,   ED. TRIBUNE."

TESTIMONIALS AS TO ITS MORAL TONE.

Dr. Edward Beecher

writes: "This book is written as a warning against yielding to temptations to crime, by showing its results in degradation and misery. It is designed especially as a warning to young men. For the sake of securing this result I recommend it to the friends of morality."

A Niece of Oliver Wendell Holmes

writes: "*Few books have so stirred my mind* for years as the book 'Forging His Chains,' by George Bidwell. Hearing of the book, prejudice immediately seized me against it. The history of a criminal, given by himself, to be interesting at all must be sensational, therefore disastrous to morals. *So avowed prejudiced thought; and, determined to find fault, I began this remarkable history.* IT IS IMPOSSIBLE TO FIND FAULT WITH THE BOOK, WHICH IS VALUABLE AND WONDERFULLY ABSORBING."

Office of Street's Insurance Agency, Hartford, Conn.

"MR. GEORGE BIDWELL : *Dear Sir*,—Some three months since, I had consultation with a clergyman regarding his son, who had fallen into bad associations and taken part in several burglaries, beside many small thefts, and seemed hardened against shame or dread of exposure. I had read your book, 'Forging His Chains,' and wrote the father as to its use in his family, at the same time securing him a copy. The boy has opened his eyes, being fully alive to the danger he has been in for a number of years, and is now supporting himself honorably. I believe the mean, dangerous boy has become a man by reading your book.   Yours very truly,   F. F. STREET."

The Rev. Thos. E. Souper,
Chaplain of the Hudson County (N. J.) Penitentiary.

"I have been a diligent reader of everything, 'ancient and modern,' but I have seldom met with anything that could compare with this *autobiography*. My estimate of this book is that it is a work of real and rare interest. But for its size, I would recommend the book to all our Sunday-schools. Indeed, I can and do earnestly commend the book to every family and household."

Pinkerton's National Detective Agency.

"I have read with interest 'Forging His Chains.' I believe it would pay every one to read this work. To any one who may harbor a desire to get money quickly, regardless of the method, 'Forging His Chains' is a lesson teaching that no matter how shrewd the operators or what good fortune follows them, the end is disgrace to themselves and to all they hold most dear. I venture to say that no person will commence to read the book without completing it. I am yours truly,   ROBERT A. PINKERTON."

See back cover.

INTRODUCTION.

DURING the past twenty years, hundreds of columns have been published in the newspapers throughout the world regarding myself and my transactions. Having been so freely commented upon by press and public, while it was beyond my power to reply, now that I am again free I feel it incumbent on me to publish the true story of the alleged £1,000,000 affair on the Bank of England in 1873, and expose the weak spot in their system.

It is now a matter of history; and as I have been regarded the principal character in that transaction, I feel sure that no one will question my ability to relate the history of this among the other events of my life. The truth herein told is stranger than fiction, and history may well be challenged to produce another life into which has come so many varied and bewildering events, or to disclose another character, trained in a religious home, having culture and an unusual business talent, free from all bad habits and the minor vices, whose deflection from the path of virtue into "crooked ways," has stirred to its very depths the entire civilized world, causing a Rothschild to tremble and the knees of money kings to quake with fear.

[Copyright, 1891, by George Bidwell. All rights reserved.]

AT HOME, East Hartford, Conn.

For the benefit of any careless reader who may fail to observe the warnings in my book, and who may fancy that he can make a fortune, or the beginning of one, by imitating the methods described in "FORGING HIS CHAINS," I wish to say:—

1st. Read my book *carefully* and *ponder* the fate of men as clever as yourself.

2d. If you still fancy *you* can commit a fraud and escape, it only proves that you have not the sense and judgment to carry out a crime successfully. Therefore, your first step would be into the hands of the *police*.

3d. The merchandise-swindling operations have become so well known that even the postmasters and freight agents would unfailingly put the police on you at once. Hundreds of men in both England and America are to-day in State prisons for attempts of the kind.

4th. In regard to letter of credit, check, and other frauds on bankers, those men named in chapter   have completely played out that game and *themselves*. The whole time I was in prison they, and others used as tools, have, until arrested and imprisoned, worked both sides of the Atlantic until now the few who are free are longing for an opening into an honest business, recognizing that any fraudulent attempt will surely land them in prison. I know two men who have squandered hundreds of thousands of dollars who have for months past been put to great straits to obtain food, not daring to try on the old games which you possibly fancy *you* could execute successfully.

5th. If (after reading my book and this note) you still cannot see that it is best to get on honestly — even if slow — then try it on, and when you are where I have seen so many thousands of like mind with yourself, you will have ample time — as they and I had — for *retrospections* and *reflections*.

If any young man will be advised, let him not squander the leisure time of his young manhood about the bars and billiard rooms, but like our physically Great Anglo Saxon progenitors, consider the first twenty-five years of life as a preparatory period. Until you are twenty-five think only of two things — how you may improve yourself physically and mentally. Then you will be ready to take advantage of opportunities that come to everyone to engage in a legitimate life-work, and at thirty-five years of age will be far ahead, in wealth and social position, of those who think they must put on full steam at eighteen or twenty, and think only of momentary pleasures, which are quite right in their proper place, as part of a mental and physical training. Your sincere well-wisher,

George Bidwell

CHAPTER I.

A BANK OF ENGLAND DEPOSITOR.

SOON after our arrival in London, Mac received an invitation to visit some relatives in the north of Ireland, with whom he was in correspondence, and invited Austin to accompany him, I being absent from London for three days. They were to start immediately, but Austin had £2,000 of my money in his pocket in bank-notes. Not liking to risk taking them along on the journey, it became a question as to how to dispose of them until his return from Ireland. Finally it occurred to him that on the way to the railway station he could call in and deposit it with his tailor, Mr. Edward Hamilton Green, of No. 35 Saville Row, he having an appointment to call there to try on a new suit of clothes that morning.

After my arrival in England, it was not long before I had occasion to offer in payment a £5 Bank of England note. The dealer handed it back, and asked me to put my name and address on the back of the note. "But," I replied, "this note is payable to 'bearer,' and requires no endorsement." However, the dealer insisted that he could not accept it unless I should endorse it. As such was not the custom in my own country, it looked to me like a piece of tom-foolery to require that notes payable to the bearer should be endorsed. Suddenly I seized a pen and scribbled on "Tom Noodle, Thames Embankment," or some other absurdity, and this was quite satisfactory to the shop-keeper. Occasionally, even when paying cash for an article in gold or silver, the shopman would ask for my name and address, with a result similar to the above. At the trial in the following year, the prosecution desiring to overwhelm us with quantity to make up for the lack of quality and exactitude of evidence, brought forward every shop-keeper to be found, from whom any of us had made purchases, in order to produce a worse impression by the number of aliases; and this sort of thing was carried so far that several witnesses made mistakes in identification, etc.

Austin's acquaintance with Mr. Green began in this wise: Soon after his arrival in England, on the 18th day of April, 1872, he was sauntering along Saville Row, taking a general view of high life at the "West End," when his eye lighted on some cloth in a shop-window. He entered the place and found himself in the presence of Mr. Green. He ordered and paid for a suit, through some freak giving the name of F. A. Warren, No. 21 Enfield Road, where I was lodging. Now there is nothing more certain than that when this occurred there was no intention of using Mr. Green for any purpose beyond his legitimate business; yet the prosecution brought this circumstance in as a link in the alleged long-prepared scheme of fraud.

The 4th of May following, on the way to the railway station, according to the plan mentioned at the beginning of this chapter, they had the cab stop at Mr. Green's. After trying on the clothes, Austin asked him to keep £1,200 until his return from Ireland. "Austin said he had more money than he thought it prudent to leave at his lodgings, and that it was about £2,000. I did not like to keep so large a sum, and recommended him to deposit it in some bank; adding that my bankers were close at hand. Austin then accompanied me to the Western Branch of the Bank of

England, where I kept an account, and I introduced him to the assistant manager, Mr. Fenwick." The foregoing are Mr. Green's own words at the trial, and he had "forgotten" a good deal which would have shown Austin's disinclination to leave the money elsewhere, giving as the reason that he should return from Ireland in a few days; but behind this was the consciousness that he was known to Mr. Green as Warren, and in case of an introduction to the bank it must necessarily be in that name.

WESTERN BRANCH.

Upon being introduced to Mr. Fenwick, Warren (as I shall call Austin in this connection) asked Mr. Fenwick to give him a simple receipt for the £1,200, which was the sum he wished to leave. Mr. Fenwick advised him to leave his signature and take a check-book, remarking that he would find it very convenient to be enabled to check for money wherever he happened to be. Warren declined accepting the

offer, on the ground that he had no use at that time for a
bank account, and repeating that he should want the money
on his return from Ireland. This was quite true, as I had
already matured my plans to go to Rio Janeiro, not having
the remotest idea of any opening in England for a "speculation." Mr. Fenwick gave further reasons why it would be
better to open account with the money than to leave it otherwise, and finally, as McDonald was waiting, he acceded to the
proposition, and started for Ireland with him.

I had no knowledge of all this until their return, three
or four days later, and I was greatly surprised when I was
told about the Warren account with the Bank of England.
Indeed, when it was first alluded to I paid no attention,
thinking, as I had a good right to do, that they were endeavoring to "take a rise" out of me. Not till the bank and
check books were produced did I give their incredible story
any credit. Austin asserted that when going to the bank
with Mr. Green, he had no idea that it was to the Bank of
England. At all events, after the matter had been communicated to me and duly considered, I could not perceive any
benefit to be derived from a continuance of the account in a
false name, and as before said, I had decided to go to Rio
Janeiro, expecting to make use of my capital there, and then
go home without returning to England. For this reason, I
directed "Warren" to withdraw the money and close the
account.

Within a week of his return from Ireland he called at the
bank for that purpose. Now mark what passed. It is a rule
of the bank of England that every depositor must keep a balance of at least three hundred pounds. Warren informed the
manager of his intention to close the account as he was intending to leave England. Upon hearing this the same arguments
that were used to induce him to open the account were again
brought forward to show him the advantages which would
arise in case the account was continued. Warren said that he
expected to employ all his money and could not leave the bal-

THE BANK OF ENGLAND. (From the Jubilee No. of *London Graphic*.)

ance required in order to keep the account open. After many pros and cons he concluded to leave the odd money — a balance of thirty-nine pounds — at the same time assuring the manager that there was no probability of his having any occasion to make use of the account. A week later I sailed from Liverpool on board the Steamship *Lucitania* for Rio Janeiro, expecting to go around the coast of South America to San Francisco, and thence by rail to New York, and the bank of England account lay forgotten until the defeat of my South American plan and return to Europe the first of September following.

At the trial the prosecution slurred over this and every other fact which would tend to show that the " Great Bank Forgery" was *not* a long planned scheme. Also, in pursuance of their theory, which they considered absolutely necessary to establish in order to clear the bank-managers from the charge of looseness in conducting business, the witnesses from the bank at the trial, on being pressed on these points, had "forgotten" or could only say to "the best of their belief," and so on. By bringing to bear their more than imperial power, unbounded influence, and the expenditure of $350,000, they succeeded in "proving" that we had been working and preparing the scheme during more than a year before the possibility of such a fraud had ever entered our heads. The success of the prosecution on that point was one of the chief causes which got us life sentences, instead of the ten years or less, usual in cases of forgery. It may be that *I* deserved even so severe a sentence as that, but surely some of the others — well, I refrain, leaving the reader to judge for himself.

To sum up the matter: The bank-books will corroborate my statement regarding the small balance lying a long time without additional deposits. The eagerness shown to have " Warren " open the account in the first instance, and the breaking of a bank of England rule in permitting the account to remain open with one-eighth of the required balance — no business being transacted during three months or more — at the time filled me with surprise, and I can now account for it only on the supposition that the Western Branch had not been long established, and that the manager, or his representative, wished to increase the business as much as possible in order to make a good showing at the head office.

BANK OF ENGLAND SCENE.— VISITOR HOLDING £1,000,000 ($5,000,000) BANK OF ENGLAND NOTES.

CHAPTER II.

BORDEAUX, MARSEILLES, AND LYONS "DONATE" $50,000—A BAD QUARTER OF AN HOUR—EGGS AND PEASANT WOMEN—"SWEETS TO THE SWEET"—A MYSTERIOUS STRANGER DISAPPEARS AMONG THE TOMBS—REUNION IN LONDON—COWARDICE OR "PRUDENCE" OF GEORGE ENGLES.

BEFORE leaving New York, Engles had come into possession of several letters of credit issued by the Bank of North Wales, Liverpool, which had been picked from the pocket of an English traveler while getting on a train in Jersey City. These the thief had discovered were worthless to him, and as there are threads of intercommunication running through all the different classes of criminals, it was surmised that though the papers were valueless to an ordinary thief, the opposite might be the case with a forger. We proceeded to make use of them in the subsequent fraudulent operations by which French bankers were victimized. I purchased a circular letter of credit from the London and Westminster Bank, one of the largest banking institutions at that time in Great Britain, the Bank of England excepted, and about the only one which did not require any reference regarding the above purchase. I next procured lithographed letter heads which were *fac-similes* of those in use at the London and Westminster Bank. In the letter of credit was a list of the bank's correspondents throughout the world, so that the traveler might get the notes which were attached to his letter turned into the currency of whatever country he happened to be in. On the lithographed letter-sheets mentioned above were written letters of introduction addressed (say) Messrs. Smith & Co., Bordeaux; Bruno & Co., Marseilles; Blank & Co., Lyons; all reading as follows:

[Printed letter heading.]

LONDON AND WESTMINSTER BANK,
LONDON, March 22, 1872.

MESSRS. SMITH & Co., Bordeaux, France:

GENTLEMEN, — A valued customer of ours, Mr. Thomas Hooker, is about to visit your city. Mr. Hooker holds our circular letter of credit, also special letters of credit issued by the Bank of North Wales. We shall take pleasure in honoring any drafts which he may have occasion to draw against these Whatever you may find it convenient to do in forwarding his business affairs, or contributing to his enjoyment, will, as occasion offers, be cordially reciprocated.

I remain, gentlemen, very sincerely,

(say) LEWIS SMITH,
Manager London and Westminster Bank.

I have forgotten the names given, and make use of any others by way of illustration. These letters were mailed in London, envelopes sealed with wax, and stamped in exact imitation of those sent out by the bank. The day they were mailed I went alone to France, having in my possession the genuine circular letter of credit with notes attached, issued by the London and Westminster Bank, and three false letters of credit purporting to be issued by the North Wales Bank, for about three thousand pounds each. All these documents had been written by George Engles.

Crossing the channel from Dover to Calais, the small, black, side-wheel steamer — a pitching, rollicking, little monster — seemed to enjoy all the discomforts of the passengers aboard. In due time I arrived at Paris, and without delay took the train for Bordeaux.

Before leaving London, letters were posted to Thomas Hooker, in care of the firms I intended to victimize in the three cities named. Therefore, on arriving at Bordeaux, I called on Smith & Co., and inquired if there were letters for me. They at once gave me the one mailed to myself, which had come in the same mail with one for their firm purporting to be from the London and Westminster Bank. The receipt of

---

NOTE — This, and other similar matters, is published as a warning to business men to verify all letters of introduction presented by strangers where money is involved.

my letter satisfied me that Smith & Co. had received theirs, which must naturally place me very high in their estimation. During my criminal career I never could avoid experiencing a certain qualm, when taking advantage of the confidence placed in me by gentlemen who received me courteously and with marked attention. But the thirst for riches, once implanted, will lead any man to unthought-of depths of infamy. As soon as these gentlemen were aware that I was "Mr. Hooker," they lavished every attention upon me — invited me to dinner, and a drive through the city afterward. I thanked them, and explained that I was obliged to decline, as my agent was waiting for me at Bayonne, where I had purchased some real estate; and having been recommended to their firm, I should feel obliged if they would cash my draft for two thousand pounds, and endorse it on my letter of credit (handing over one on the North Wales Bank). Mr. Smith replied that it was the custom of the French bankers to require twenty-four hours' notice before drawing a check, and asked me if the next day would not answer. "We shall be happy to assist you," said he, "in passing the time pleasantly." This was a new custom to me, but I answered instantly, expressing regret that the nature of my business precluded delay, it being necessary that I should reach Bayonne that night. "I suppose," continued I, "that your bankers will not mind your checking out a small sum without the usual notice. However, if it occasions any embarrassment or inconvenience, I can easily procure the money elsewhere." One of the partners replied that their bank would without doubt honor their check, and the matter should be attended to at once. I sat down for a half hour, conversing on a variety of topics. Of course this was a most trying period to me; the least show of haste or anxiety might have betrayed me to those lynx-eyed, experienced men of business. In the midst of our conversation, an undercurrent of thought kept running through my mind, thus: "Who knows but they have sent a dispatch to the London and

Westminster Bank, merely as a matter of business precaution, and that they are delaying me to get a reply? In that case, I shall have a good opportunity to learn the pure French accent, while passing my days in the Bagnio at Toulon." At last, however, the amount was paid over to me in French bank-notes. I deliberately counted them, and took leave, lighter in mind, and heavier in purse by fifty thousand francs.

I had arranged with Engles (whose merits for a criminal calling in the way of cowardice were described in a former book) to go every morning to the Queen's Hotel, London, for letters which I should send addressed to "H. Cowper."

After receiving the money, I enclosed it in a large envelope, addressing it to Cowper, London. I also wrote on the envelope: "Echantillions du papier" (*i. e.*, samples of paper), after which I posted it at the post-office.

As I wished to reduce the risk as much as possible (the train for Marseilles not leaving for three hours), I took a carriage and told the driver to carry me towards the next station on the route to that city. After we were fairly out in the country, I got outside and sat with the driver, discoursing with him about the country we were driving through, arriving in the village about half an hour before the train from Bordeaux was due. I dismissed my driver at a small village cabaret or tavern, walked to the station, got aboard the train, and early the next morning was in Marseilles. I breakfasted at the Hotel d' Europe, and looked over the papers to see if the Bordeaux fraud had been discovered. As I could see no indication of it, about 10 A. M. I took a carriage and went to call on Messrs. Brune & Co.

Here, as before, I found a letter for Mr. Hooker, which assured me that they had received the bogus one addressed to themselves, consequently every thing looked clear for the fresh fraud contemplated.

On making myself known I was, as usual, received with the utmost courtesy, began to talk business, and one of the firm got into my carriage and rode with me to his bank to effect the sale of my draft on London for the sum of £2,500. Arriving at the bank I took a seat in the front office, while Mr. Brune went into the manager's room to introduce the transaction; the clerks eyed me as I thought suspiciously, but doubtless only curiously, because they perceived I was a foreigner. Another thing which I noticed sent a shiver through me. After Mr. Brune had been a few minutes in the manager's room, the bank porter stepped to the outer door, closed and locked it. It being but 12 o'clock, I imagined the precautionary measure must be due to my presence. "The Bordeaux affair is discovered and has been telegraphed all over France," was my first thought; "all is over with me. I am a candidate for a French prison, sure. My poor wife! My poor children! Alas! what a fool have I been!"

These and a thousand other thoughts flashed through my mind during the quarter of an hour preceding Mr. Brune's reappearance with his hands full of bank-notes. I could hardly believe my eyes. I had suppressed all signs of the internal hurricane which raged during those prolonged moments of suspense.

Now the revulsion of feeling was so great that I nearly fainted. However, by prodigious mental effort, I recovered my self-possession and effectually masked all inward convulsions.

Mr. Brune placed in my hands sixty-two thousand francs, in notes of the Bank of France, and we then descended to the carriage and drove to my hotel, where, after mutual expressions of esteem, I, a base swindler, separated forever from a victimized and honest man. I paid my bill at the hotel and at once made preparations to start for Lyons, which was to be the next and last scene of my operations in France.

As my train did not leave for three hours, I got into a carriage at some distance from the hotel and was driven towards the next station, located on the beautiful bay a few miles from Marseilles.

After driving along the shore of the bay for some miles I remember we met two women, dressed in the quaint costume common to that part of the country, each carrying a basket of eggs. I stopped the carriage and endeavored to enter into conversation with the pair, but could not understand a word of their *patois*. I then took a couple of eggs, handed out a silver franc piece, and drove on, leaving two astonished women standing in the road, gazing alternately at the piece of money and at the back of my carriage. Arriving at the station I found it would be an hour and a half to train time, and driving to a hotel on the shore, I ordered dinner to be served in the upper room of a two story tower overlooking the bay, with Marseilles in the distance. After dining I strolled along the beach, looking at some queer fish, not found north of the Mediterranean, their colors vying in brilliancy with the plumage of tropical birds. Returning to the station I took a ticket for Lyons, stopping off at Arles about sunset, as I wished to see the ampitheatre and other relics of the Roman occupation.

I sent a dispatch to Lyons addressed to myself (Hooker), care of Messrs. Blank & Co., as follows:

"T. Hooker: Bring sixty thousand francs to Arles at once, as I have completed the purchase.   C. E. Hooker.

It will be seen what use I made of this dispatch. I remained in Arles till midnight, then took the train arriving in Lyons at nine the next morning. Repairing to the Hotel-de-Lyons I had breakfast, and on looking over the papers, became satisfied that as yet no discovery had been made. Therefore I resolved to carry out my third and last financial enterprise, and then return to London with all speed.

I called a carriage and drove at once to the establishment of Messrs. Blank & Co. Here I found a letter from London and the dispatch from Arles. I sat near the desk conversing with the head of the firm as these were handed me. I opened the letter and found nothing but a blank sheet of paper, having forgotten that one of them had thus been sent. I saw the merchant's eye on it, and remarked in an explanatory way, "I see, it is written with sympathetic ink," and put it in my pocket. I then opened the dispatch sent from Arles, and after reading, handed it to him saying: "I see that I shall have use for sixty thousand francs, and must ask you to cash a draft on my letter of credit for that amount." He immediately stepped to the safe, took out a bundle of one thousand franc notes, and counting out sixty gave them to me, I, of course, signing a draft on the London and Westminster bank, and having the amount endorsed on my forged letter of credit.

As it was almost certain that the Bordeaux fraud would soon be discovered, I determined, now that my dishonorable work was completed, to attempt an immediate escape from France, by way of Paris and Calais. I did not, therefore, take the train direct from Lyons to Paris, but engaged a carriage and drove back to a junction toward Marseilles. Here I took a train which intersects farther to the northward with another road leading through Lyons to Paris. After going the roundabout route above described, I was back at the Lyons station at 9 P. M., in a train bound for Paris, where I arrived without further incident.

The next morning (Sunday) as I left the railway station, I thought detectives were watching me, but in all probability it was only the imagination of a guilty conscience. I was then wearing a full beard, and as a precautionary measure I that morning had all shaved off save the mustache. Not daring to leave Paris on the through express, which started at three o'clock P. M., nor to purchase a ticket to either Calais or London direct, I went to the station, and took the noon accommodation train which went no farther toward Calais than Arras, a town some thirty miles from Paris. I arrived there about one P. M.

As it would be about three hours before the express train was due I went to a small hotel and ordered dinner. To while away the time I took a stroll through the main street, where were many mothers and nurses with children, nice black-eyed French babies. As I was always a devoted lover of children and other small creatures, I stepped into a shop and bought a package of confectionary, which I distributed among the little ones and their smiling nurses, receiving therefor, almost invariably, the grateful exclamation, " Merci, Monsieur !" I gave some to children eight and ten years old, a crowd of whom soon gathered about me. Perceiving that I was attracting too much attention, it was clear that I must get rid of my young friends as soon as possible, or the police would also be attracted, and their presence might lead to unpleasant results in case the frauds had been discovered and enquiry was being made for an " Englishman." Purchasing a second supply of candies I hastily gave them out, and with a " *Restez ici mes enfants*," I passed through them and continued my walk up the street. Quite a number followed at a respectful distance, and I was cogitating how to double on them when I came to the gateway of the town cemetery, through which I hastily entered. The children remained outside and watched me as I walked up the slope and disappeared. At the rear of the cemetery I observed an old man at work in the adjoining field. I climbed upon the stone wall, which instantly crumbled away, and I was landed on the old Frenchman's domain without leave, amidst a pile of stones. Startled by the racket, he looked up from his digging, and, seeing a stranger uprising from the ruins of the fence, began consigning him to " *le diable*," with a volley of vigorous French expletives delivered in peasant patois. I listened to him much amused for a moment, and then held up a five franc piece. As soon as he beheld it a wondrous change came over him. He eagerly seized the silver and straightway showed me to a lane which led almost directly to the railway station. I purchased a ticket for Calais and took the Sunday afternoon express, arriving in London the next morning, after an absence of but four days. The money procured in Lyons I had with me, but the one hundred thousand francs sent by mail without registry I was uneasy about. I therefore hastened to find my companions to ascertain if the letters had been received at the Queen's hotel.

Engles had been left in London to secure the money-letters at the hotel as fast as they should arrive. But he had been afraid to go there and inquire for them, and when I reached London, I was thunderstruck at his rather too extreme caution. I immediately took a valuable hand-bag filled with linen, etc., went direct to the hotel, registered the name to which I had addressed the letters, asked if there were any letters for me, and they were all handed over forthwith. I had the lady clerk assign me a room, and left my bag. I then walked leisurely away, and have never been back for the bag to this day. The principal reason for leaving Engles in London was to give him an unobstructed opportunity to exchange the foreign bank-notes into English gold before my first bogus draft should arrive, for as soon as the detectives were put on the fraud, they would go at once to all the London Exchanges and broker's offices to watch for any one who offered large sums in French notes. Owing to his pusillanimity I had been obliged, after returning from my trip to France, to undergo the additional hazard of calling at the Queen's hotel. Engles having thus failed to act his part, we were encumbered with a large amount of French paper and a bag of foreign gold which could not be offered safely for exchange in London. I therefore decided that Engles should go to Paris, accompanied by one who had played no part in the fraud, as an assistant, leaving myself, the guiltier one, safe in London. They accordingly left at once, Engles taking the bag of gold, and his companion the notes. The latter afterwards informed me that, during the whole journey from London to Paris, Engles sat with the bag of gold under his coat, ready in case of any imagined emergency to throw it out of the window or overboard while crossing the channel. After their arrival in Paris the assistant was obliged to do the whole business, not only of selling the gold but also the notes.

While he was in different brokers' offices—for he did not dare to offer a large amount in one place—Engles stood at a distance, ready to run away at the slightest indication of danger. However, they arrived safely back in London with the proceeds of my three days' nefarious work in France.

And thus ended—viewed from the forger's standpoint—perhaps as brilliant a "solo" operation as has been recorded in the annal of crime.

Surely this chapter ought to cause business men to act very cautiously in dealings with strangers, even when they come provided with introductory letters. When credit, money, endorsements, or identification at a bank or other business house are asked on such letters, quietly step to the telephone or telegraph and verify them. This plan has become of common usage among knaves. Do not expect to see villainy depicted in the faces of this class of *business men*—for such they regard themselves, having been usually brought up as such.

Chapter III.

"THE TERROR OF WALL STREET" RETURNS TO NEW YORK—TAKES PARTIES OF FORGERS TO ENGLAND AND THE CONTINENT—HE IS ARRESTED—FRUITLESS EXAMPLES—STARTS A FARO BANK—FIGHTS STRANGE "TIGERS"—HIS PREMATURE DEATH IN 1886—VOYAGE TO RIO JANEIRO—THE LADY OF THE LUCITANIA—A SWEDISH COLONEL'S PARTY OF ENGLISH ENGINEERS—A BIBULOUS CHAPLAIN—$50,000 ON BOGUS LETTERS OF CREDIT—MR. SOLOMONS—AN ANXIOUS TIME—MUNSON IN A "FIX"—STRATEGIC MOVEMENTS TO EXTRICATE HIM.

ENGLES remained in London about a week, preparing forged papers for me to use on the trip to South America, which was already decided upon, and then took steamer for New York from Liverpool. On the same day I sailed for Rio Janeiro, accompanied by one known in this adventure as Munson. Since my return from England I have heard some particulars of Engles' life and death since we parted in Liverpool.

In 1879 Engles sent a party to England who took over drafts forged by him with which they procured $40,000 from Seligman & Co., bankers, London. Our party were sentenced for life, as a warning that Engles and Wilkes should not attempt their operations in England. But I have ascertained that during the time I was in prison, not a year elapsed that one or the other did not either go over or send a gang with forged paper, prepared by them in New York.

In 1880, in company with Wilkes, Hamilton, and Burns, Engles went to Italy, where all but himself were arrested, Burns killing himself while in prison.

Hamilton and he were chained to the wall on opposite sides of the room. Wilkes' confession plunged Burns into a state of desperation. He seized upon a prayer-book, lay down, and bending the covers back he placed two corners each side of his wind-pipe and pressed so hard that he choked to death.

Hamilton from his side of the room gazed upon this fearful scene, at first too horror-stricken to act, then began screaming and shouting madly for assistance, but none of the Italian jailers were aroused by his frantic efforts until after his friend had accomplished his purpose.

And we were incarcerated for life as a warning to prevent forgers from coming into Europe! I think that I have remarked elsewhere that the imprisonment of one person seldom has any " warning " effect upon others, because no person takes part in a crime committed to obtain money, unless he feels sure that his arrangements are such as to secure his escape — despite all examples to the contrary, each one believes himself the one who will not be caught.

As stated, Engles escaped from Italy and was arrested, but for want of proof the extradition case against him failed, and United States Commissioner Osborne discharged him from custody. He had, however, lain in the Ludlow Street jail over twelve months, during which time the case against him was in progress. In 1884 he made up another party, going to England himself, and obtained a large sum on forged paper.

On every occasion some of the men were arrested and imprisoned for presenting the forged paper. While in prison, at different times, I had word sent to me by prisoners that they were in for presenting forged paper, and that they had come to England with Engles. Two of them were Hebrews of respectable birth, natives of Poland, who had lived in New York for several years. When arrested they were sharp enough not to let it transpire that they were from America, in consequence of which they got off with five years' penal servitude, instead of the fifteen, or life sentences, which would have been given them had it been known that Engles had brought them to England.

In the relation of Engles' European operations, I have somewhat anticipated my story, and will resume it with his arrival in New York in 1872, and his establishment of a faro bank in that city. His peculiar reputation among the "crooks" of America brought to his place many people ambitious to fight the "tiger." He would soon have become a second John Morrissey, had he only been able to restrain his own propensity for drink and gaming; but these habits had now become so firmly fixed that he was no longer master of himself. He had a great many "ropers-in"—those who lounge about the hotels, make acquaintance with merchants and other visitors from the country, and entice them into gambling-houses and other dens. A "roper-in" is a well-dressed, plausible-speaking man, one who has the faculty of conveying to strangers the idea that he is one of themselves; and is paid one-half of all the money he can, "by hook or by crook," induce his dupe to disburse at the various dens visited. Such gaming-houses as the one in question pay these pimps one-half of all the money "won" from their *protégés*, they acting as mentors and advisers to their confiding dupes. In consequence of this mutually profitable arrangement, Engles gained a great deal in the way of "winnings" at his own faro bank, but soon tired of playing, in effect, against himself, for whether losing or winning, there was no risk of ultimate loss. Therefore, he could feel none of that peculiar excitement, kept at fever heat, which had become necessary, and which he had experienced while throwing his ill-gotten gold lavishly into the jaws of some other gambler's "tiger," especially those at that time on exhibition at the splendid establishments of the "Honorable" John Morrissey in New York, and at Saratoga during the fashionable season. At these were lost most of the large sums procured by the extensive gold forgeries in Wall Street and elsewhere. Engles was the only gambler with whom I ever had anything to do, as I considered it especially dangerous to do any "crooked" business with the assistance of either gamesters or drunkards.

It was now the same as it had been with the large sums obtained by forgery, for all the booty raked in at his own establishment was immediately staked and lost elsewhere, regardless of the claims of an affectionate wife and children. His taste for brandy had so grown upon him that he required, more and more, the stimulus afforded by that potent fluid, and was constantly under its influence. His originally strong constitution succumbed at last to the long-continued strain, and he died miserably, after a year's sickness, in 1886, leaving his family impoverished. His wife is carrying on a small business near New York, and endeavoring to bring up her children to become respectable members of society.

The reader's attention is now directed to the steamship *Lucitania*, of the Pacific Mail Line, ploughing the waters of the rough "Bay of Biscay, O." While she is rapidly approaching the coast of France, I will relate what preparations were made in London to carry out the object of our voyage. While "Warren" was settling up his account, though leaving a small balance at the Bank of England as previously described, Engles had busied himself in completing the forged letters of credit that I was to take with me on our voyage. These purported to be drawn and issued by the London and Westminster Bank. In filling them out he had signed only the manager's name, but as I had noticed that in the "circular" letters of credit issued by that bank, both that and the sub-manager's name were signed, I argued that the same should be done in regard to the "special" letters. But Engles insisted that one name was sufficient, because, as he stated, he had seen several genuine letters of credit of the same description, which had been issued by the Bank of North Wales, Liverpool, with the manager's name only. Nothing could induce him to put on both names, although he might have done it in a few minutes, and he being an "old head" in the business I was reluctantly obliged to give way. As will be seen in the sequel, the want of acumen shown in this instance by my usually astute confederate, saved the good bankers of

South America, in all probability, a million of dollars, defeating my project at the outset, and causing us to return to England contrary to our wishes or expectations. It may be curious to note here, as an instance of how slight a thing may change the whole future life of a man, that this decision of Engles not to spend five minutes in putting on another name, led to the discovery of the plan to make use of the Bank of England account, and all that followed. And this, besides the narrow escape (about to be recounted) from passing our lives on the island of Fernando da Noronha, which lies in the Atlantic about three hundred miles off the coast of Brazil. On this island is located the one great convict establishment to which are transported the convicts of the Brazilian Empire. Both on the voyage and return the steamer passed within sight of it, and on each occasion the view excited within me very curious feelings — in going, the thought that, despite my precautions, we might find the end of our journey there — and in returning, the thought of our narrow escape from being there instead of on board the steamer in the enjoyment of all luxuries.

To resume — the good steamship *Lucitania* rapidly neared the mouth of the Garonne, or Gironde, on an estuary of which is situated the old city of Bordeaux. Arriving there, she lay at anchor for some hours, taking in and discharging freight, and receiving emigrants for various parts of South America. When the steamer was about to leave, it was a strange and rather comical sight to witness the farewells and leave-takings from the crowds of friends who had come to see them off. The customary performance appeared to me so peculiar that I will describe it as well as I can after so many years: Two men standing face to face, one clasps the other round the body, the other passive, then leaning back lifts the party clear off the ground once, twice, or thrice, probably according to the degree of relationship or amount of affection; then the operation is reversed, the embraced becoming the embracer. In some cases the ceremonial is repeated the second or third time, neither kissing nor crying being the fashion there.

The next morning we were off the coast of Spain watching the silvery gleam from the ice-clad peaks of the Pyrenees — at least those of us who were not engaged in the more disagreeable employment of discharging their debt to Father Neptune. However, by the time the ship arrived at the small port of Santander the passengers were mostly recovering from the *mal de mer* occasioned by the rough water in the Bay of Biscay. While leaving this tiny land-locked harbor, one of the propeller blades touched the rocky bottom and broke short off, but she continued her voyage with undiminished speed, and within three days was steaming up the Tagus to Lisbon. Here the passengers who wished to avail themselves of the opportunity, had a few hours on shore, then we were off for the long diagonal run across the Atlantic, unbroken save by a call at one of the Canaries.

" The Lady of the *Lucitania*," as she was called, because there was no other lady among the saloon passengers, was the wife of Captain ——— of the British army, who was going out for a few months' hunting on the pampas of Buenos Ayres, and of course accompanied by numerous dogs, with an assortment of guns. There was also a chaplain in the British navy who was going out to join his ship at Valparaiso. A strange character was he; being a big, burly man, about 28 years of age, and the most inveterate champagne-drinker on board, and that is saying a good deal. Whenever he met any of the "jolly" ones of the saloon passengers it was "Come, old fellow, will you toss me for a bottle of phizz?" as he called his favorite wine, and he had no lack of accepters. The majority in the saloon consisted of a party of fifteen young Englishmen, civil engineers, who were going under the leadership of a Swedish colonel to survey, for the Brazilian government, a railway line across the southern part of Brazil, from the Atlantic to the Pacific. In all there were twenty-five young men, full of frolic and fun, who made matters rather lively about the afterpart of the ship. They went in for every thing from which any fun could be extracted. At the equinoctial line they roped in the "greenhorns," of whom I was one, to look through the field-glasses at the line, and having fastened a hair across the field of view, of course we could all see it plainly. Father Neptune came on board, and those of the crew who had never crossed the Equator were hunted out of their hiding places, dragged on deck, lathered with a whitewash brush dipped in old grease, shaved with a lath-razor, and then tumbled unceremoniously backward into a cask of water.

THE "SUGAR-LOAF" IN THE BAY OF RIO.

During the whole voyage I laughed, and increased in weight twenty pounds. After a prosperous voyage of three weeks we arrived within sight of the famous "Sugar-Loaf," and were duly disembarked at the custom-house, where I found it indispensable to use a little "palm-grease" in order to get my baggage through that institution without a long waiting. The evening succeeding our arrival a banquet was given at the Hotel d'Europe, which was attended by most of the saloon passengers, including "The Lady of the *Lucitania*."

The next morning Munson called at a banking-house, presented his false letters of introduction, and was well received. He immediately commenced business — showed them a letter of credit, and making out a bill of exchange, drawn on the London and Westminster Bank, he sold it to the banker, and drew ten thousand pounds in the currency of the country, leaving the balance on deposit as the nucleus of a bank account. I had been waiting outside, and saw him come out with the currency — a package a foot square — under his arm. At some distance from the bank he gave me the package, and I took it at once to an exchange office and purchased English sovereigns for the whole amount — about $50,000. On the voyage, Munson and myself had acted as strangers to each other, and now we stayed at different hotels, being careful not to be seen together, meeting in the parks or other public places, though in isolated parts of them. Having bogus letters to other bankers in Rio, this first easy success satisfied us that we could obtain all the money — say two or three hundred thousand dollars — that we should think it prudent to ask for in that city.

After the lapse of two days, Munson again called at the same bank and was immediately invited into the manager's room and introduced to "Mr. Solomons," a Hebrew, who proved to be one of the leading brokers on the Rio Exchange. As before, I was waiting outside, and owing to the long time Munson was in the bank, I began to feel uneasy, and surmised that something was going wrong. At last he made his appearance, and I saw by his flushed face that he had been under a strain. Upon reaching a suitable place, he related to me the particulars of the interview. The danger we were in no doubt tended to indelibly impress upon my memory Munson's statement, which was in substance as follows:

"The manager, after introducing me to Mr. Solomons, said that a short time previous a letter had been received from the London and Westminster Bank which stated that from that date all letters of credit issued by them would be signed both by the manager and sub-manager. He then said that the letter on which he had purchased my bill of exchange had but one name. The Hebrew broker sat all this time with his crafty eyes fixed upon me, as though he would read me through, and it required all my nerve to enable me to stand the situation without showing signs of uneasiness. I replied that really I could not say how the omission occurred, but I supposed it must have been accidental, and then told him I would look at my other letters and see if they were the same. Mr. Solomons said it was a very singular circumstance that an assistant bank manager should neglect to sign a special letter of credit, still he must have done so; but for his part he should not feel justified in purchasing bills on such letters. After some further conversation, the manager asked me if I had letters to other parties in Rio. 'Certainly,' said I; 'I have letters to the English Bank, and to Messrs. —— & Co., both of whom have doubtless had advices from their London correspondents regarding me, and I will ascertain at once whether I am to have the object of my long journey hampered by the neglect or oversight of the sub-manager.' I then came away. The fact is, I am feeling very shaky; the Hebrew is a shrewd old codger, and the manager refused to purchase any more exchange on London on the pretext that he had all he could use. This is awful! I had a hot time of it, and no mistake! That Solomons is as sharp as a razor, and as suspicious as a boarding-house mistress. I think he is assured in his own mind that something is wrong. I am afraid it is all up, and I wish we were well out of this country."

"There can be no doubt about it," I replied; "and at this moment they are doubtless consulting as to what measures can be taken to secure the ten thousand pounds paid you until they can get advices from England. The cable is not yet completed, and they must wait the slow movement of the mail, which will take forty days. You informed him that you expected to remain in Brazil three months, and as it is known that no one can get out of the country without getting his passport viséd at police headquarters, they will not arrest you for fear that after all it may be only a mistake, unless you attempt to leave Brazil. A bold step must be taken. Here are the other letters of credit; take this pen and write in the sub-manager's name."

Although Munson was a skillful penman, he had never attempted to forge names himself, Engles having performed that delicate operation during the short time we had been in such business. The ordeal through which Munson had passed had made him nervous; therefore, though not a drinking man, I procured a glass of brandy, which he swallowed. In a few moments he began to write in the names, though with rather a shaky hand. When finished, I compared them with the genuine signature in my possession, and found it very shaky; but we were in for it, and I could see but one way out; therefore I selected the best, handed them to Munson, and said:

"It is not an hour since you left the bank. Take these letters back immediately, and show the manager *both* signatures, remarking at the same time that the second name must have been unintentionally omitted from the one on which you drew the ten thousand pounds. He cannot fathom that you could have forged the sub-manager's name in so short a time. See if it does not prove a 'poser.' Though it may not wholly allay suspicion, it will give me time to make and execute a plan for getting you out of the country. Of that I am certain. Rely on me, keep cool, and above all keep a stiff upper lip, and act up to the character you have assumed. Be sure to offer them more exchange on London, as I wish to ascertain how they take the proposition; and if they decline to purchase, say that you will have to transfer your account to the English Bank of Rio."

Starting on his decisive errand, followed by me as before, he was not long in the bank, but reappeared empty-handed, no one following to "shadow" him. Upon meeting at the designated place, Munson informed me that the manager was evidently agreeably surprised when he was shown the letters with both signatures; nevertheless, he had refused to purchase any more exchange, but had transferred the endorsement from the letter that had but one signature to one with both. All this convinced me that his suspicion was fully aroused. It was therefore clear that our safety depended upon the invention of a plan by which I could get Munson out of Brazil, and at the same time convince the bank manager that he intended to remain. It must be a plan which would throw off any one attempting to watch his movements, and make it appear that he was still in the country until the steamer in which he sailed should have been at least twenty-four hours at sea.

This plan, and how it was successfully executed, will be detailed in the following chapter.

Chapter IV.

TECHNICALITIES OF BRAZILIAN LAW — IN A TIGHT SPOT — I RESOLVE ON A BOLD COUP — EFFICACY OF A SUITABLE "DOUCEUR" — A "DOCTORED" PASSPORT — A DETECTIVE ON TRAIL, WHO INGRATIATES HIMSELF INTO MUNSON'S CONFIDENCE — MANEUVERS — THE DETECTIVE ON A "WILD GOOSE CHASE" — SAFELY ON BOARD — A DISTINGUISHED PARTY IN A ROWBOAT — A STERN CHASE — OFF AT LAST.

WHETHER the law remains the same as it was in 1872, I am unable to state; but at that time every person desiring to leave Brazil must be provided with a passport — if a foreigner, one from his own government — if a native, one from the Brazilian. When ready to start, he must take his passport to police headquarters and have it viséd, then leave it with the ticket-agent where he buys his ticket. This agent, after ascertaining from the chief of police that the intending passenger is not "wanted" by the authorities, transmits the passport to the purser of the steamer, who, in turn, hands it to the owner after the ship is at sea. It will be seen that these regulations render it very difficult for any suspected person to leave Brazil by the regular channels of communication; and if difficult for a native, how much more so for a stranger, ignorant of the country and its language, the Portuguese. French, Italian, or German, did well enough in the large towns, but the moment a fugitive who did not understand their language got into the country, he would stand a poor chance of getting far away from Rio. Therefore, I was obliged to abandon the project of going south to Buenos Ayres — a journey by land of fifteen hundred miles — or of crossing the continent to the Pacific by way of the Amazon. At last I determined on a bold *coup* to get Munson away on a steamer which was to leave on a certain day. Accordingly, I had an American (U. S.) passport filled in with the name Gilmore, by which I was known during the voyage from England, by the agent of the steamship line, and others in Rio. This I took to the police headquarters, and finding the anteroom crowded with people, I supposed I should be obliged to wait my turn; but presently the interpreter came along, and, presumably, judging by my appearance that time was more valuable to me than a little money, he whispered in French: "If you are in a hurry, you will save time by sending in a small 'douceur' to the chief, or you may have to wait all day." I took the hint and slipped into his ready palm a few reys, with which he disappeared into the inner room. In a short time I was ushered in and my passport viséd without my being troubled with an interrogation. Proceeding to the ticket-agent I delivered up the passport, receiving and paying for a saloon passage to Liverpool. He recognized me as one of the party who had arrived a few days previously by the *Lucitania*, and expressed some surprise at my early return, it being the best part of the year for a sojourn in the tropics. I explained that having completed my business, I was in a hurry to get back to my own country. My next move was to walk along the water-front and find where row-boats with oarsmen were to be let. As these were to be had at several points, I selected the most obscure one toward the northern boundary of the city. Here I found a boat, and was rowed out to the steamship *Livingstonia*. I went on board and found the purser, to whom I showed my ticket, and asked him to assign me a state-room by myself. Having paid him the extra price required for the privilege of being the sole occupant, I received the key, took a good look around, that I might find the room again without the necessity of making inquiries, and left for the city, after informing the purser that I should remain on shore until the hour for sailing the next day. Upon meeting Munson I requested him to call at the bank and casually inform the manager that he should start the next morning for S. Romao, a town in the interior of Brazil, to be absent a week. He was then to go to the Hotel d'Europe, pay his bill, at the same time stating that he was to leave Rio by the four o'clock train the next morning. As Munson had two trunks, and other *impedimenta* befitting a man of his pretensions, it was necessary to take a carriage to the station, which was nearly a mile distant. It would be unsafe to go in a carriage belonging to the hotel; therefore, he was to say that a friend would call for him. As it was still two hours to sunset, I suggested that after he had arranged matters, he should saunter out, walk about the streets until dark, then return to the hotel and be ready when I should call for him at three o'clock the next morning.

After these arrangements we separated, I following to ascertain if he was being watched or shadowed by detectives. When he entered the hotel I remained within view of the entrance. It was not long before he reappeared and walked leisurely along the street, with gold-headed cane, and real diamonds flashing in the tropical sunlight. A few seconds later I saw another man come out, cross the street, and go in the same direction. I followed him, and was soon satisfied that he was keeping Munson in view. This sort of double hunt was kept up until dusk, when Munson returned to his hotel, unconscious that a moment later his "shadow" entered the place. Here was a "stunner" and no mistake, though it was no more than I had anticipated as among the possibilities; still, I had indulged in the hope that the bank would rely entirely on the passport system, and take no further steps for a day or two, which was all the time required to carry out my plan. Though Munson had good nerve, it was already somewhat shaken, and surely the situation would have unnerved most men. Therefore, fearing that the certain knowledge of imminent danger might still further confuse him and cause some false move, I determined to keep my discovery to myself. Leaving Munson and his "shadow" to their own devices at the hotel, I next proceeded to an obscure part of the town, and stopping at a small but respectable looking tavern, I engaged a room for the next day. I also engaged a carriage, with an English-speaking driver, to be in readiness at three o'clock the next morning — then returned to my own hotel for a few hours' sleep. Promptly at the hour I was at the livery stable, where I found the carriage ready, and was driven to the Hotel d'Europe. Sending the driver up to the office on the second floor, Munson soon appeared and informed me that he had promised to take to the station a man who was stopping at the hotel. "He is going to S. Romao.by the same train," continued Munson, "and seems a good fellow, for I had a long talk with him last night." Upon seeing signs of disapproval in my face, he explained: "Well, you know, he said he could not get a carriage at so early an hour in the morning, and I thought it could do no harm to take him in, and he is waiting up stairs."

It would be difficult for the reader to imagine the effect of this surprising communication upon my mind, for it was clear enough that this was the very person who had been "shadowing" Munson the day before, and had skillfully ingratiated himself into his new friend's confidence. I could but admire his unwonted "cheek" in asking a contemplated victim for a ride to the station. I said to Munson: "What in the world can you be thinking of? Don't you see you are blocking our whole plan? Go up and tell him your carriage is loaded down with luggage, and express your regrets that you cannot accommodate him."

This Munson was obliged to do, though with repugnance, it being against his nature to do anything that looked "mean." During this time the baggage was being placed in the carriage, and as soon as Munson had dismissed his "passenger," who for some reason, did not show himself to me, we started rapidly for the station. On the way I requested him to avoid making any new friends until he should find himself well out at sea. Said I, "It might be fatal to attract the attention of any one, or to let any one see you leave the train. Of course this new acquaintance of yours is only a countryman, but it is not possible to foresee what disaster the least mistake or want of caution might originate. Now listen: if you will be guided entirely by me, you will be safe on the broad Atlantic to-night. You know," I continued, "that these cars are on the English system, divided into compartments. You must go into the station, stand near the ticket-office until your new acquaintance comes; then observe if he buys a first-class; if so, you take a second, and *vice versa*. Pay no attention to him, and let him see you get into your compartment, but keep an eye on his movements. In case he comes to get in where you are, despite the different class of the tickets, tell him the compartment is engaged. Everything depends on how you carry yourself through the next twenty minutes. A single false step, a word too little or too much, will surely prove fatal to us both!"

In accordance with our pre-arranged plan, I stopped the carriage opposite the station, it being still dark. Munson alighted, went straight inside; and in a few minutes saw his " passenger " come puffing in, nearly out of breath. Unquestionably supposing Munson's baggage to be already on board the train, he purchased a ticket, and after seeing his intended victim enter a compartment, got into another himself just as the train began to move. This was the vital moment for which Munson had been waiting, and having previously unlocked with his master car-key the door opposite, he stepped off on that side, hastily crossed to the other platform of the dimly-lighted station, and made his way unnoticed into the street. While this was passing I sat in the carriage, and it was not many minutes before I had the satisfaction of seeing Munson coming back to me. For the benefit of the driver we then had a dialogue somewhat as follows:

"It is too bad! Our friends have not arrived; what shall we do?"

"Well, I suppose we must go back to the hotel and wait for the afternoon train," I answered.

"But I have paid my bill there," said Munson, "and do not care to go back."

"Then," I replied, "meet me at the station, and I will look after the luggage."

In case they recovered the trail, the information obtained from the driver would cause confusion and delay sufficient, I hoped, to enable me to get Munson out of Rio.

I then told the coachman to drive into the city. It was not yet daylight, but after a while I saw a sort of eating-house and tavern combined, and had the carriage halted there. Alighting, I entered, and said to the person in charge that I did not wish to disturb my friends at so early an hour, and would pay him for taking care of my baggage, as I wished to discharge the carriage. This offer was of course accepted, the baggage housed, and the carriage dismissed. In the meantime Munson was waiting for me in an appointed place not far away, where I joined him, and we went to the obscure tavern where the room had been engaged.

So far my plan had been successful. Munson was hidden safely away before dawn, while at the same moment his very clever new friend was some miles distant on a "wild goose chase" into the interior. Arriving back at my hotel soon after daylight, I took a leisurely breakfast, after which I sallied out and engaged two stalwart slave porters, whom I found, according to the custom of their class in Brazil, busily occupied in plaiting straw for hats while waiting for a job. Motioning them to follow me, I led the way to where Munson's baggage was stored. Dividing it between the two, we proceeded to the place I had selected as the safest to get off to the steamer without attracting notice, and had it put into a boat. Paying the porters, I followed and was rowed off to the steamer. The baggage was hoisted on deck, the trunks deposited in the hold, and the smaller articles carried into my state-room; after which I went ashore to await the hour of the decisive movement for which I had made such elaborate preparations. There was no train by which the detective could return to Rio until late in the afternoon; and I felt certain that when he should ascertain that Munson was not upon the train, he would be confident that his intended victim had slipped off at a way station in order to make his escape into the interior. Under this impression he would naturally make inquiries at the likely stations, and even if he sent a dispatch to the bank, it would doubtless be to the effect that his quarry had left Rio on the early train that morning with himself.

The baggage had taken up my time until ten A. M., and returning to my hotel, I packed into a knapsack as many bags of gold (about £8,000) as I could conveniently carry, called a carriage, and was driven to where Munson had been waiting in great anxiety for several hours. Taking him in, we were not long in reaching the place of embarkation, and were rowed about five miles up the harbor, where the steamer had gone to take in coal. Amid the usual confusion attending the departure of an ocean steamer, we got on board unnoticed, and went direct to the state-room. By the time we were in it the gold had become excessively heavy, and I was glad enough to stow it away in one of the berths. We had not been long in the state-room before we heard the welcome sound of the bell, warning all who were not about to make the voyage to leave the steamer. I parted from Munson, recommending him to remain in his state-room until the ship should be well out into the Atlantic. Getting into the boat again, I was rowed away a short distance, then had the oarsman rest on his oars, and soon had the pleasure of seeing the *Livingstonia* glide past with her prow pointed toward the "Sugar-Loaf." Now, for the first time, I breathed freely, and felt a great weight of responsibility roll from my shoulders. "Munson is safe, and the danger is over," said I to myself, joyfully. Ordering the boatman to row ashore, he turned in that direction, and then I saw a boat coming toward the steamer, with every oar strained to the utmost — but no attention was paid to it. The occupants soon gave up the chase, and through my field-glass I recognized the manager of the bank and the Hebrew broker, Mr. Solomons, both of whom had been pointed out to me. They had probably just received a dispatch from the detective who had been so cleverly outwitted and left to journey alone, but having no time to procure an order to delay the ship, had hurried off, hoping to get on board, confident that the captain would grant every facility for a search, and, in case of success, assist them to get Munson on shore again. Had they succeeded, I should have been involved, and probably learned the lesson on the island of Fernando da Noronha that I did later in England.

CHAPTER V.

IDLE DAYS AT RIO — IMPERIAL HONORS — VISIT TO A COFFEE PLANTATION — SLAVES — A TRIP TO THE LA PLATA — TEN DAYS' QUARANTINE ON THE ISLAND DE FLORES — MONTEVIDEO AND BUENOS AYRES — THE "LA FRANCE" — OUT IN A PAMPERO — RETURN TO ENGLAND.

DURING my stay in Rio Janeiro I received from the Swedish Colonel, before alluded to, an invitation to be present at a special presentation of "Ernani" at the grand opera-house in honor of the Imperial family, in accordance with which I became one of the favored audience. This was very small, and appeared to be composed of the *creme de la creme* of Brazilian society, the Imperial box being occupied by the Emperor Dom Pedro, the Empress, their daughter and son-in-law, the latter having made his name famous in Brazilian history by his gallant conduct during the late war between the gigantic Empire of Brazil and the liliputian State of Paraguay. At the Academy of Fine Arts in Rio I noticed a large painting representing him seated on a fiery war-horse plunging about amid shot and shell, the princely rider, with sword waving on high, guiding the storm of battle. The Imperial family formed a marked contrast with the remainder of the audience, being plainly dressed and making no show of diamonds or other jewels.

Now that Munson was safely on the broad Atlantic, with the bulk of the gold in his possession, I felt at ease, though there was still a chance that when it became certain that he had made his escape out of the country, I might be regarded with suspicion and detained. But as I had been extremely careful not to be seen in his company, I felt no great anxiety on that point.

The great mistake of that period of my life was that I did not abandon every other plan and go at once to Chicago to establish a legitimate business, in accordance with my original intentions.

After securing all the cash we safely could at Rio, Munson taking the leading part, we had intended to go down the coast to Montevideo and Buenos Ayres, and repeat the operation, I doing the leading business in those cities. Going thence by steamer *via* the Strait of Magellan to Valparaiso, we were to continue northward, stopping at the large sea-ports along the Pacific Coast as far as San Francisco, from which place we intended to reach New York by the trans-continental railway, with at least a million dollars in our possession.

It will be seen that this was a gigantic and well-devised scheme, which might easily have proven a complete success — my experience having led me to believe that such expectations were by no means unreasonable — had not Engles's obstinacy thus frustrated our plan. In yielding to him the point that came up in London, as to whether both the manager's and sub-manager's names should appear on the forged letters of credit, I acquiesced in a step which virtually defeated the whole scheme, and changed an easy money-making affair into what just missed turning out a tragedy.

After due consideration, I could see no way of getting out of Brazil otherwise than by a voyage to the Rio de la Plata (river of silver), it being supposed that I had sailed for Europe on board the last European steamer; in consequence I had to keep myself secluded as much as possible, to avoid running against the Pacific Mail·Line agent and others.

As it would be some days before I could obtain passage southward, I passed the intervening time in making excursions and sight-seeing, Rio and vicinity being a good place for both. I need not weary the reader with an extended description of the beautiful bay of Rio, closed in on all sides by mountains which rise almost from its shores, with the unique Sugar-Loaf, 900 feet high, like a huge sentinel guarding the entrance to a harbor which vies with the far-famed

SCENE NEAR RIO JANEIRO.

bay of Naples in the natural beauty and grandeur of its situation and surroundings.

The approach from the sea is very attractive. First

appear distant peaks, scarcely distinguishable from the clouds. Approaching, the outlines become more distinct, and other mountains become dimly visible in the distance, while the hills and slopes are covered with luxuriant tropical vegetation. Until the steamer nears the land, it appears as if she is about running against a solid wall; but when quite near, the cleft through the mountains opens up, and as she enters this, a part of the city appears in the distance. On the north side, opposite the Sugar-Loaf, is the fort of Santa Cruz, on which is a lighthouse; other fortifications guard the harbor, and no obstruction prevents ships from entering it in safety day or night. The water in this land-locked harbor is deep enough and its area sufficient to accommodate all the navies of the world.

The Sugar-Loaf seemed so near the city that I thought it would be a good day's sport to climb to the summit, and accordingly hired a boat with two oarsmen to row me down to its foot. After a long row, to my surprise it appeared as far away as ever; and as I could not understand the jabbering of the boatmen, I reluctantly gave the signal to return. A visit to the Horticultural Gardens, with their rows of gigantic palm-trees, and every variety of tropical flowers and plants, was exceedingly enjoyable; but nothing could be finer than a drive along the sides of the mountains behind the city, not more than a half-hour's ride from its center. Here were located the villas of merchants and bankers, almost hidden by the foliage of shrubs and trees, and commanding a view of both city and harbor.

One day, with an acquaintance, I took the early train on the same line where the detective was perhaps still looking for Munson, and alighted at a small hamlet on the border of a stream, about thirty miles from Rio, beyond the mountains. Calling at the only store, we found no one able to speak either French, Spanish, Italian, or German. Happening to look across the street, we saw a sign reading, "Schroeder, Painter." We hurried over, and entering, received in answer to my "Sprecken sie Deutsche?" a "Ja, mein herr."

With the painter's aid, as interpreter, we were soon mounted on horse and mule respectively, I taking the latter. My companion intended to be considerably amused at my efforts to make the mule keep up with him; but he counted, on that occasion, without a proper knowledge of the character of that particular mule, which proved the better horse of the two. .

We rode for some miles through a country covered with mound-like hills, no sooner coming to the bottom of one than we were ascending another. These hills were covered with coffee bushes, filled with red fruit about the size of cherries, each containing two kernels. The coffee was being picked into large flat baskets by slaves, which when filled they carried away on their heads to the drying ground. The roads were bordered with orange trees loaded with luscious fruit, to which we helped ourselves. After a time we turned into a bridle-path, and rode three or four miles through a dense forest. We emerged upon the outskirts of a coffee plantation, where the slaves were just on their way to dinner; and another half-mile brought us to the planter's residence. Thirty or forty slaves of both sexes and all ages were grouped upon the grass, engaged in eating a black looking stew out of metal dishes, their fingers serving for knives, forks, and spoons. Seeing two horsemen ride out of the forest, they stared in stupid wonder, until one, more intelligent than the others, went in search of the overseer. Presently a white man appeared, and to our question: "Parlez vous Francais?" shook his head. "Sprecken sie Deutsche?" another shake, and the same to "Habla Espagnole?" but, on hearing, "Parlate Italiano?" came the smiling answer, "Si, signor." He proved to be an Italian overseer, in charge of this plantation owned by a merchant in the city, who seldom visited the property. The overseer showed us over the place and explained all the processes of preparing the coffee for market.

In one corner of a large, unpainted wooden building was what he called the infirmary, and a comfortless looking place it was. He said there was no doctor employed and that he dealt out medicine to the slaves himself. After being served with coffee, we departed and returned to Rio by the evening train.

As the south-bound steamer was due the next day, the question which occupied my mind was: "How am I to get out of Brazil?" Munson had left me his passport, from which I erased his name and description, and put in my own. The next morning I hired a person to take my passport to police headquarters, grease the official palm, and have it viséd, although the chief was by law obliged to compare each passport with its holder. He soon returned with the document in proper shape, and I then purchased a ticket, leaving the passport with the agent. I embarked without trouble, and in four days was laying off Montevideo, at the mouth of the Rio La Plata, waiting for the health-officer. At that time there was no telegraph cable, and everything went slow along the coast of South America.

After keeping the steamer waiting for some hours the health-officer condescended to come aboard, and although there had not been a single case of sickness, to declare us in quarantine. Accordingly, after discharging the river freight, she ran out to sea thirty or forty miles to the Isle de Flores (flower island), on which the passengers were landed and kept there ten days, paying three dollars per day for board. At the expiration of this tiresome period we were taken on board a small steamer and landed at Montevideo.

In that beautifully situated city of revolutions, the windows are barred like those of a prison, and the walls beveled so as to enable the inmates to shoot up and down the streets.

Taking the night steamer, I was landed at Buenos Ayres (good air) the next morning. At that time the place was a mongrel between the oriental, tropical, and a brand-new western town. After a few days I determined to return to Europe. Therefore, my proper name being in my passport, I purchased a ticket for a passage by the steamer *La France* to Marseilles.

Running up the coast of South America we were in a pampero (hurricane) for twenty-four hours; and although the *La France* was one of the largest steamers then afloat, the waves dashed away over her smokestack and tossed her about like an empty cask.

The *La France* ran into the harbor of Rio Janeiro and lay off the city for several hours. When she came to anchor a sidewheel steamer of the line which ran from Rio to New York was at the point of leaving. I hailed a boat and was rowed off to her to ascertain if I could secure passage to New York. When my boat reached the side of the New York steamer, I was informed that nearly all passenger accommodations had been secured for the Brazilian Prince Imperial, and that I could not be permitted to come on board.

What slight circumstances may change the destiny of men for better or for worse,—for a life of poverty and wretchedness or prosperity and happiness,—for a long life or a premature death! Had I been able to proceed direct to New York, and from thence to Chicago, to carry out my long-deferred plan, my whole destiny would have been changed; for the possibility of perpetrating the frauds on the Bank of England was then among things unknown, and afterwards discovered only by accident.

Among my baggage I always carried a galvanic battery, and as there were several hundred Spanish, Portuguese, and Italians in the steerage — none of whom had any experience with electricity, as developed by human agency — we had no end of sport by tempting them to take a silver coin out of a bucket of electrized water, and by playing many games to give them unexpected shocks. These people were ignorant and superstitious and soon came to believe that we were in league with the devil.

In due time I landed at Marseilles, took the train for Paris *via* Lyons, and arrived in Paris where I joined Munson. In the next chapter will be detailed the series of operations which led to the disastrous affair with the Bank of England.

Chapter VI.

I MEET MUNSON IN PARIS — HIS ACCOUNT OF THE VOYAGE FROM RIO — A PLEAS-
URE TRIP TO VIENNA — ORPHEUS AND EURYDICE — AN ELECTRIC PHENOMENA —
I AIR MY GERMAN — RETURN TO LONDON — INCIDENTS OF TRAVEL IN GERMANY.

AFTER my return to Paris I met Munson, who related to me the incidents of the voyage from Rio Janeiro, and subsequent events. The following is an epitome of his story:

"For some little time after you left me on board the *Livingstonia*, I remained perfectly quiet in the state-room, until I heard the screw begin to revolve and I felt satisfied that the steamer was at last under way. I then ventured out on deck, and recognized you in the boat. I also, through my glass, saw a boat at a distance pulling hard toward the steamer, and the sight made my heart give a great thump; but as the steamer continued on past the last fort, headed for the ocean, I recovered my equanimity and drew a breath of relief, you may be sure. Then, for the first time, I realized what a terrible strain I had undergone for the week previous to my escape from Rio Janeiro. It was just the tightest bottle I was ever corked up in, and had I known of those regulations about passports, I never should have put my neck so nearly into the Brazilian halter; and when we were passing the lonely island where the convicts are kept, I gazed upon it, happy that I was no longer a candidate for a long residence in that desolate-looking place. On board I found everything correct, and no suspicion existing that I was not the man who had purchased the ticket.

"When we were about two hundred miles out the engine broke down, and for a time I thought she would have to put back to Rio. In that case I knew it would be all up with me, and you can imagine the state of my feelings while the suspense lasted. However, after a few hours the break was repaired, and we got under way again.

"The $40,000 in gold, which I kept in my state-room, was a source of much anxiety. I hardly dared to go on deck, or into the saloon at meal-time, through fear that it might be stolen. At last I put the money in possession of the purser, who charged me two per cent., or eight hundred dollars, claiming that it was the regular rate. On the arrival of the steamer at Lisbon, I determined to go on shore, and make my way to Paris overland through Spain, for the reason that I feared dispatches might have been sent from the nearest cable station to England, warning the police to be on the lookout when the steamer should arrive at Liverpool.

"As the gold was too heavy a load to lug about, and likely to attract attention, I went to an English firm of brokers doing business in Lisbon, and purchased Portuguese stocks. Having thus got the money into portable shape, I journeyed by rail and diligence to Paris, where I have since remained."

A few days later I met McDonald. He was eager for "business," and almost the first question he asked was, "What is the programme?"

"Let us return to the United States," I replied. "We have a good capital now to put into a straight mercantile business. Let us do no more 'crooked' work, which will be certain to get us into trouble sooner or later." For that "one more operation" among all classes and grades of thieves, from the common sneak to the colossal bank defaulter and "boodler," is continued until the small ones get into prison, and the great ones (generally) get out of the country.

We finally concluded to go to Paris and Vienna for a time. When we reached the latter city we were delayed by the sickness of McDonald, who was suffering from a disease like modern "malaria." I nursed him for two or three weeks, and during the time gave him several powerful shocks.

from my battery, which nearly raised him out of bed, if they did not cure him.

We were living in Vienna—McDonald at the Golden Lamb, and I at the Grand Hotel. While waiting for Mac's recovery I visited the Imperial opera-house almost nightly, and never tired of listening to the music of the magnificent orchestra — then the best in the world — each member being a solo artist or professor, and receiving a large salary or pension from the Emperor. The operas were rendered in the German language, and "Orpheus and Eurydice" was brought out in a manner that left an indelible impression upon my mind, although I had previously witnessed that great creation of Glück's in Paris, London, and New York.

As I passed the entire day with McDonald at his hotel, I must have contracted his malady to some extent, for when he began to get about I was prostrated and confined to my room for a whole week. As I had never experienced serious illness of any kind since childhood, I became so impatient by the end of the week that, notwithstanding the doctor's commands, I declared myself recovered, got up and dressed myself for a walk. On each floor of the Grand Hotel in Vienna there was at this time (1872) an office where a servant or two was in waiting to answer the bells. When I was ready to go out I had occasion to call a servant, and touched the electric button. I distinctly heard the bell in the office ring in response, as I stood, cane in hand, waiting at the open door of my room. Soon I touched and held down the button for a longer time, and again waited in vain. In my then nervous condition I lost both patience and temper, and continued the pressure on the button with the following result: My room was located in a back corridor farthest from the office. When I touched the button I heard the electric bell connected with my room tingling rapidly; soon another joined in — then another — and another — until I had a concert of at least a hundred bells going. Presently servants came rushing through the corridor, and seeing me, one of them explained that my bell had set all the other bells in the house going, and in consequence they could not tell what room the call was from. I could only tell them that if they had answered my first or second call there would have been no concert. Thenceforth my calls were promptly answered so long as I remained at that hotel. Had Mark Twain been at the Grand Hotel that day, I am sure he could have obtained material for an entire humorous chapter.

While on the way to Mac's hotel I used frequently to stop in at a news-office to purchase the daily paper, which I read assiduously to improve my knowledge of the German language. This news-office was conducted by two sisters, who were fair specimens of their sex in a city famed the world over for beautiful women. I used to air my German by asking in that language for the papers I wanted, and generally, to my great satisfaction, found that they understood me. After I had been a regular customer for some time, I ventured to attempt a compliment upon the good looks of one of the sisters, remarking: "Sie sind schon!" A look of surprise and the exclamation "Was?" (what) caused me to repeat in my best German: "Sie sind schon!" The young lady blushed, looking at me earnestly, and seeing that I wore an innocent air and was apparently unconscious of anything but pride in my knowledge of German, cast her eyes thoughtfully downward for a moment, and then suddenly burst out laughing, clapped her hands vigorously and said: "Oh Meinherr! Sie wollen sagen schön!" (You are beautiful). The reader will observe the two dots (diaeresis) over the "o" of the last "schon," without which the pronunciation of the word is quite different, and signifies "already" instead of "beautiful." I had no intention of saying to her, "You are already!"

Of the many incidents connected with this Vienna trip, I distinctly remember two. While on the train between Paris and Frankfort—having no money current in the German States —I could purchase nothing to eat. . This was before the new Prussian coinage had displaced the wretched system previously in vogue, by which each petty State manufactured its own circulating medium. In the same compartment with me was a Hungarian gentleman and his wife, on the way from Paris to their home in Prague. This gentleman spoke English fluently, and as soon as he learned that I was an American, both himself and wife became enthusiastic in their efforts to be sociable. Noticing that I did not get out at the halting places for meals, he finally inquired the reason. When I acknowledged the dilemma I was in, he produced a large pocket-book, which he opened and handed to me saying: "Help yourself." From a large amount in Austrian bank-notes I selected one of the smallest denomination, and returned the pocketbook with my thanks. On arrival at Frankfort, I at once procured the amount at the hotel and sent it to the courteous Hungarian.

On another occasion, at the station of a German town, a young married couple came into the same compartment. They appeared to belong to the prosperous portion of the community, and a throng of well-dressed people came to the train to see them off. The bridegroom wore a big, loose German wrapper, something like an ulster, and I observed that the pockets were like bags well filled. Not long after we came to a dining station, where all but the bridal pair and myself had dinner. I naturally supposed that the excitement of the occasion had taken away their appetites, but was thoroughly undeceived when, a little later, the man spread a newspaper over their laps, took from one pocket a loaf of bread at least one and a half feet long, and from another a monstrous bologna sausage. Then, taking out his pocket-knife he cut off a "chunk" of each for his bride and for himself. In a remarkably short period they had eaten fully one-half the provisions, and the remainder was consigned back to the pockets until supper time.

I mention these incidents of travel merely to illustrate the proverbial generosity and honest simplicity of the Slavonic and Germanic character.

CHAPTER VII.

UNSUCCESSFUL ATTEMPT TO "BEAT THE DUTCH"— MAC'S "GREAT DISCOVERY" — LONDON AGAIN — FIRST INCEPTION OF THE GREAT BANK OF ENGLAND FORGERY — DEDUCTIONS FROM MCDONALD'S "GREAT DISCOVERY" — VERIFICATION OF COMMERCIAL NOTES AND BILLS OF EXCHANGE — LETTER FROM A BANK MANAGER — I CABLE TO AMERICA FOR NOYES — SIR SIDNEY WATERLOW'S CLERKS — MISTAKEN IDENTITY — A KEY TO THE MYSTERY — NO WOOD ENGRAVERS IN PARIS — I PUT MY NECK IN THE HALTER — HORTON ACCOUNT OPENED AT THE CONTINENTAL BANK — THE "FRAUD MACHINE" IN WORKING ORDER — I RESOLVE TO GIVE UP THE CONTEMPLATED FRAUD AND GO HOME — A FATAL COMPLIANCE — DON'T.

ONCE more in London with my two companions, the question arose: "What next?" I had determined to abandon a dangerous business; but difficulties arose which caused delay in the execution of my project, until finally I concluded to go to Amsterdam to see if I could find an opening for one more operation which was to be the very last — and such the one opened up by this journey proved to be. Leaving my companions in London, I arrived in the city of dykes and canals, and at once began prospecting among the bankers. But the cautious Hollanders would have nothing to do with strangers at any price, no matter how plausible the pretext. It was in vain that I showed them my circular letter of credit and United States passport. These awe-inspiring documents, which elsewhere had proved a sufficient introduction, had no effect with the good burghers of Amsterdam. They received me very politely, and on my expressing a wish to purchase a bill of exchange on London (or any other city), the reply invariably was: " Have you a letter of introduction to us?" Upon my replying in the negative : " We never transact business of any kind with persons unknown to us," was added in way of explanation. Then handing over the documents above mentioned, I said: "Unfortunately I did not procure letters to any one in this city, not expecting to make any stay, but I suppose my letter of credit and passport will be a sufficient introduction for the purchase of a bill to be paid for in cash?" "Anyone can procure a circular letter of credit," was the reply; "besides it is our invariable rule to decline all dealings except with those with whom we are acquainted, either personally or by introduction." A few trials with the same result satisfied me that some other plan must be discovered. I was nearly at my wits' end as to how to insert the small end of the wedge which should pry out a good-sized nugget from the "pocket" of one of these bulky — in body and estate — but justly cautious Hollanders, who really understood how to do business safely.

Some time previously I had purchased several bills of exchange in Frankfort, drawn on merchants in Amsterdam, but not yet due. I now called on them, and, in each case, had the bills accepted, at the same time telling them that I wished to use the money and would feel obliged if they would pay their bill at once less the discount. The reply was as I expected, that they based all their merchandise operations on paying bills only as fast as they became due. The real object of the request was that I should have some excuse for asking the address of a broker whom I could employ to purchase bills, etc. My ruse was successful—for, supposing that one who held their own paper to a considerable amount must be all right, upon my request a member of one of the firms on whom I called gave me the name of a Mr. Pinto, a Hebrew member of the Amsterdam Stock Exchange. In this way I soon procured several addresses. With the list I returned to the "Black Eagle," and after a twelve o'clock dinner I went in search of Mr. Pinto and found him at his residence — a front room of which served for an office — in the Juden Strasse (Jew Street), and a strange place it is on a Saturday afternoon, the time when I first visited that unfragrant quarter. Informing him of my business and the name of the mer-

chant who gave me his address — which he appeared to think
a sufficient introduction — he took the matter in hand, and
leaving 20,000 guilders in Dutch bank-notes with him for the
purchase of bills on Hamburgh, also the Frankfort bills before
named, to be sold on "Change," I departed. Calling the following day I found that he had accomplished the transaction.
I then deposited a still larger sum with him, and requested
him to purchase some bills in "marks banco." These were
duly purchased and delivered, but so far I could see no opening for a "speculation" of my peculiar kind. Having no
particular plan of procedure up to this moment, I was only
casting about in an experimental way. A day or two later I
called, and arranged to have him sell on Change all the bills
on Hamburgh. Later he informed me that the rate of
exchange on that city was lower and that he had not sold on
account of the price. Upon explaining that I had another
operation in view that would recoup me for the loss, he immediately went on Change and sold out at a loss of fifty
pounds sterling. Among the bills previously purchased was
one on Baring Brothers, which I had sent to McDonald in
London, and which, as will be seen, proved to be the first step
in the "Great Bank Forgery."

Aside from the Barings bill the purchase and sale of all
those bills had accomplished nothing but to increase my
respect for the cautious, therefore safe modes of transacting
business in Holland. In these respects, far ahead of any
other country in which I ever had business transactions, the
strict uncompromising methods of the Dutch rendered the
country a most unfruitful field for all classes of swindlers.
I had sold out the bills as above, because there seemed to be
no possible way, that I could see, to "beat the Dutch," and I had
in consequence resolved to proceed to Frankfort-on-the-Main,
with the hope of finding some way to make the Rothschilds
contribute a small part of the wealth accumulated at the original starting-place of that remarkable family. My preparations for going to that city being completed, at the moment of

departure I received a dispatch from Mac that changed the whole aspect of affairs, and proved that the unpremeditated sending of the Baring bill gave the first impulse to a train of ideas which finally culminated in the fraud on the Bank of England. Let the reader bear in mind that this was in November, less than four months before the first false bills were sent to the Bank of England for discount. The dispatch read as follows:

LONDON, November 2d, 1872.
To GEORGE BIDWELL, Amsterdam:
Have made a great discovery. Come immediately. MAC.

This dispatch was really the first inception of the fraud; and yet the bank managers, in order to protect themselves from the charge of carelessness, although aware of the existence of the dispatch, made every effort to carry the impression that we had contrived the plan of the fraud in America; had there spent many months in making preparations; and that all of our operations on the Continent, described above and elsewhere, were a part of the original scheme. I have no desire to extenuate or excuse, but this fact, together with the alleged "attempt to escape from Newgate" during the trial, was what really got us the "life sentence."

That dispatch was a great mystery to me, but I quickly decided to obey the summons, first obtaining through Mr. Pinto a number of bills of exchange drawn on first-class London houses. Arriving in London the following night, I received from McDonald a solution of the mystery. I give his explanation, as near as I can remember, in his own words:

"As soon as I received that bill on Baring's I went there to collect the money. Instead of paying the amount by check or in gold or notes, as I expected, the cashier stamped on the face: 'Payable at the London and Westminster Bank,' and endorsed it. Upon taking it there it was cashed without a question. It occurred to me immediately that if we were to get some blank bills of exchange, we could make as many as we liked by imitating the original, and draw the money from the bank with the same ease that I did for the genuine bill."

Such was the "great discovery" that had brought me from Holland, and it might have worked for the small sums that could be drawn in one day, with due regard to safety. That did not suit me, and Mac's financial plan was never put in operation in the form he had conceived; nevertheless it served as an initiatory step in the long journey which we were preparing to undertake.

McDonald had no sooner informed me of the particulars regarding his "great discovery" than it flashed through my mind: "Here is the opportunity to use the long-neglected Bank of England account." I reasoned that as the bank had paid the Barings bill to McDonald without verifying the signature, it must be the custom in England to transfer bills of exchange from hand to hand without sending them to the acceptors to be initialed. If this was true, it followed that the banks discounted paper without making any inquiry as to the genuineness of the signatures, relying entirely on the character of the customer who offered the paper for discount.

Here was an opening, indeed!

When this proved to be a fact, all I had to do was to start a manufactory for making imitation bills, and deposit them in the Bank of England for discount through the medium of the "Warren" account.

This reasoning appeared to be sound; still, I could not believe it to be among the possibilities that any bank, especially an institution like the Bank of England, should do business in so loose a manner. In New York, so long ago as 1854 — the year of my first visit to that emporium — it had been the custom among the bankers and brokers to send all offered paper to the purported drawers or acceptors to have it initialed by them. In consequence of that very necessary precaution, any attempt to perpetrate on a New York bank such a fraud as the one so easily carried out against the Bank of England, would have been nipped in the bud.

The following letter from the London *Times* comes in *apropos* at this point:

LONDON, September 8, 1873.

To the Editor of "The Times":

Sir, — The revelations which have been made, in connection with the late Bank of England forgeries, have shown us a weakness in our way of doing business in neglecting to obtain the verification of acceptors and drawers to bills discounted.

Doubtless the presentation and initialing of every bill discounted by our large London bankers would entail much time and extra labor, and would in many cases be impossible; but it would be a comparatively easy matter to send a copy of each bill discounted to the acceptor and drawer, informing them that such a bill had been discounted by Messrs. ———, printed forms being kept for the purpose, leaving a blank place for name, date, and amount.

I am, etc., BANK MANAGER.

In turn I explained my plan of using the Warren account in the Bank of England that had been lying so long comparatively useless. Without delay the bulk of our money was placed in Warren's hands to deposit in the account, so that in case we finally concluded to attempt the execution of the fraud, the large balance would show well on the bank books. I also sent the following cable dispatch to E. Noyes ("Noyes"), New York:

Come by first steamer. Answer, Langham, London.

In sending for Noyes at this time, my idea was to have "Warren" introduce him to the bank, and let him open an account, by means of which the fraud could be carried on, leaving Austin entirely disconnected with it, save in having introduced Noyes. I imagined that in such a case no proof could be adduced that he knew, at the time of introduction, of Noyes' intention to defraud the bank. On more mature reflection I saw that such a transfer might thwart the whole undertaking, by starting inquiries which should bring to light the very slender foundation on which the Warren account had been opened with the Bank of England. Besides, that account had been made more solid by the length of time it had been opened, and the amount of legitimate business transactions through it. I therefore proposed an alternative plan which was at once put in execution, as follows:

On the 2d of December, 1873, Austin, who had not yet had the warning of a portending railway accident, opened an account at the Continental Bank in the name of C. J. Horton, depositing £1,300 in bank-notes. As anticipated, seeing their new customer deposit such a sum, no embarrassing questions were asked by the managers, and, doubtless, noting that he had "business" transactions with a depositor in the Bank of England, whose checks were duly honored there, they were led to believe that further inquiry was unnecessary. The next day I had a Warren check deposited to Horton's account, and the operation repeated, varied with checking out small sums, from day to day, in order to give the affair an air of genuine business. I also purchased several bills of exchange, and had Warren take them to the bank manager, Mr. Francis, for discount. Upon returning from the bank, he said there would be no risk in taking £50,000 in false bills and bringing away the gold, thus ending the whole matter at a stroke. But this appearing to me a hazardous undertaking, I adhered to the slower plan, though, as the sequel shows, such a *coup* might have been successful. The backs of the bills were covered with the endorsements of the various firms through whose hands they had passed. These endorsements were copied in *fac-simile* so that the false bills in contemplation should have all the characteristics of the originals.

As bills of exchange will be frequently mentioned, some of my readers may not know exactly what they are, and how used. For example, a manufacturer of silk in Lyons sells goods to the amount of five thousand dollars to a responsible merchant on six months' credit. The merchant gives his note or bill for the whole, or, as is usual, several of five hundred or a thousand each, to the order of himself, or the manufacturer, payable at (say) Rothschilds' in London. He is careful to see that his balance is sufficient or to arrange with the Rothschilds to accept and pay them when due. The manufacturer endorsing pays them out, or puts them in his bank for discount. The bank in turn also endorsing, sells them to a customer who has bills to meet in London. After endorsing, he likewise remits them to his correspondents, who pay his bills with the proceeds of their discount or sale—first, however, sending them to be accepted by the Rothschilds, from which time they are known as " acceptances."

It may be easily seen how I was enabled to plan and execute this mammoth fraud, when I state that the Bank of England cashed acceptances such as I have described without sending them to the Rothschilds to see *whether their signature or acceptance was genuine.* The last seven words give the key to the whole mystery. While in Germany I had purchased every variety of ink on sale at the stationers, so that in case of need I could have not only any written document imitated, but also written with like ink. I had also, out of curiosity, purchased a great variety of blank bills of exchange, printed in French, German, Dutch, Italian, Russian, Turkish, and Arabic. At the time of this purchase, my companions laughed at me for " lugging about a lot of trash " for which I had no possible use. But, now that I was about to tackle the Bank of England, I found them, like Mrs. Partington's coffin-plate, handy to have in a portmanteau. I also continued sending remittances to my Hebrew broker in Amsterdam, Mr. Pinto, requesting him to send me several bills on London. These, together with some already in my possession, gave me the opportunity of getting a great number of the endorsements, stamps, and signatures of leading firms on the Continent and in London.

I went to the printing and stationery establishment of Sir Sidney Waterlow, then Lord Mayor of London, before whom we were afterward under examination at the Mansion House, at intervals for four months (see cut), there I left an order for two books of blank drafts or bills of exchange, and in a few days called at the city office for them. The manager had to send to the printing-house for them, and in consequence kept me waiting more than an hour, he and the clerk talking with me for some time. Yet those two men within three months swore before their master, the Lord Mayor, on our examination, that McDonald was the man — he having light hair and blue eyes, my hair being black — and Mac and I sitting beside each other in full view of the witnesses.

I only mention this as an instance of mistaken identification, which less than fifty years ago might have hanged Mac, and set me, the real actor, at liberty. In this connection it will be proper to state that, not wishing any one to suffer for my own acts, as soon as the day's examination was over, after returning to my lonely cell in Newgate, I wrote a full account regarding my visit to the Lord Mayor's establishment, giving particulars which proved so conclusive that those important witnesses did not appear at the subsequent trial at the Old Bailey.

I also required some small wood engravings — fac-similes of the various bank and private endorsement stamps. It had been a part of my plan that I was to remain in the background, contriving and giving directions, leaving others to carry them out. The reason for this was that I might be free from anxiety for my personal safety, and would thereby be enabled to act with coolness and judgment in the management of the business, and in disposing of the proceeds of the fraud in case the project should be successful. I also intended that no one of us, except Noyes, should show himself in England in connection with the affair, therefore I sent McDonald, who could pass for a Frenchman, to Paris to get the required blocks engraved. After three or four days' absence he returned to London without them, and gave me the surprising information that there were "no wood engravers in Paris." I afterwards discovered that while there he whiled away the time, and returned to play that tale on my credulity.

Placing implicit belief in that statement, I had a serious argument with myself as to whether I should not throw up the whole matter and go home, rather than do anything which might involve me and leave a possible clue to connect myself with the fraud; for it would be a very delicate operation to procure the blocks, etc., in London, without arousing suspicion, and I would trust no one else to do it. Suppose that the actions or words of the person sent should excite the suspicion

MERCHANTS EXCHANGE, ILLUMINATED.

of the engraver, trifling indications of which might not be noticed, or thought worth reporting to me? The engraver would communicate his suspicions to the police, detectives put on, and we "ambushed" in the midst of our operations. Finally I resolved to order the blocks myself — *there being no wood engravers in Paris*—though with great reluctance, and with the feeling that I was committing a grave error. I therefore made a list of all the wood engravers in London, and spent two or three days driving about in a cab, selecting five out of the forty or fifty with whom I conversed, to do the work, judging them to possess simple, unsuspicious natures. The result proved that I made no mistake in my selections, as the work was quickly done, and no suspicions as to its real object transpired.

It would appear that the qualifications thus worse than wasted, if properly used might have taken me to the top round of the ladder; though I do not mention this in a boasting spirit, but only to show that where I made a failure of getting rich by dishonest means, others would doubtless have been defeated, for "something" always happens.

In the meantime Noyes had received my cablegram and sailed for England. An hour after his arrival in London I met him, and in answer to his inquiries, informed him that I was speculating on the Merchants' Exchange, and expected to wind up my operations shortly. I told him he must ask no more questions, but follow my directions implicitly and promptly; that I should not even let him know where the rest of us lodged, after the first of January. I further informed him that he was to act as clerk for "Horton," and though our operations were a little irregular, that he should be taken care of, kept out of danger, and be well paid for his services; and impressing it on his mind to obey orders like a soldier, I left him.

And yet, this man, who was to be paid with about five per cent. of the proceeds of the crime, received the same life sentence, and is at the present time serving his nineteenth year at hard labor in Portsmouth Prison, England. When arrested, *he would not betray us!* even though the prosecution offered to permit him to turn Queen's evidence, the acceptance of which would have freed him as soon as the trial should be finished. Let his case be a warning not to touch pitch lest ye be drawn into the slimy depths.

In order to secure Noyes against any fatal disaster in case of a premature discovery, I had an advertisement for a situation as clerk, by one who could deposit a cash guarantee, inserted in the Daily Telegraph (London). This Noyes was to show to the landlord of Durant's hotel where he was staying, and arrange a meeting between himself and Horton, taking care that persons should be within hearing while the latter bargained with the former to become his clerk. To cover this source of danger to Noyes more surely, I had them go to David Howell, solicitor — of whom more anon — who drew up an article of agreement between them, for which that delectable limb of the law charged ten pounds sterling. On December 28, 1872, I mailed from Birmingham to the Bank of England genuine bills of exchange, amounting to four thousand three hundred and seven pounds, for discount, in order to ascertain if our "Fraud Machine" was in working order, and as they were discounted without question, this proved to be the case.

Shortly after the events just recorded, I received a letter from my wife which determined me to return home at once, and woe to me that I failed to carry out that determination. Going immediately to the Grosvenor Hotel, where my two principal associates were staying, I informed them of my resolution. After some discussion it was agreed to drop the plan against the Bank, and I reverted to my old idea of going to Chicago to engage in trade.

Upon leaving I told my brother that I was going to pay my bills, and should call later for a check for my share of the money in the bank. Having paid up all my personal debts, I found that I could get off to America by the next day's steamer from Liverpool. Permit me right here to call attention to one of those very slight causes which affect a man's entire future existence, and which made me change my plans, so that, instead of passing happy years amidst family and friends, I came to endure long years of misery in a foreign prison. Thus it happened: While I was absent, McDonald

requested my brother Austin to propose to me that I should
leave my share of the money behind in the bank and draw
for it after my arrival in America. Accordingly, when I
returned, that proposition was made to me, and it placed me
in a quandary; for I did not like to show apparent distrust
by refusing, nor did I like the idea of leaving it behind.
Besides such a proposition at that juncture, made me suspect
an intention on their part to remain behind with the idea
of attempting to carry out the plan of fraud. In my opinion, any attempt to undertake the management of such an
operation, involved certain disaster, as neither of them possessed the exact qualifications requisite, especially an exact
knowledge of, and experience acquired in, legitimate business. I theorized thus to myself: "This is one of those
unique operations which, if anything, will result in a great
success or a terrible disaster. I see clearly that the affair
can be carried on so that only one person need show himself,
and if each does his part thoroughly, it can be done with
little or no risk. Still it will not be common prudence for us
two brothers to take part in the same criminal operation. If
I go into this, he shall go home; and if I should get into trouble, he could look after my family. But that 'if' is what
troubles me. To be sure, I can shroud the operation and
the operators in so thick a veil of mystery that it would
trouble them to get a clue or even to discover the fraud until
two months after we should all be out of England." It will
be perceived that the whole plan and system of operations
stood clearly outlined in my mind. One thing alone gave me
cause of distrust, and that was the possibility of carelessness
or neglect on the part of my ablest associate; but I thought
I could make such strict terms and conditions that no
disaster would be likely to happen from that source, *unless
I was directly deceived* and kept in the dark regarding his
movements, and I believed he had too much good sense to do
that. The result will show, by one of the most remarkable
examples on record, that the only road to final success is to

keep clear of the slightest contact with wrong-doing, no matter how plausible the reasonings.

Certainly, in planning so gigantic a fraud, I believed every point could be so completely covered, that even my name would never be known, for otherwise I should have been hunted through the world. Without this apparent certainty I should have abandoned the idea of a job which turned out so badly that it took me nearly fifteen years to get out of it.

If among my readers there may be one who has become possessed with the idea that he cannot make money enough honestly to satisfy his desires, and is inclined to try the other plan, my counsel is — *don't!* Better to reduce the desires to fit the circumstances, than get into circumstances the end of which may be a prison — in any event, disgrace.

I tried one plan thoroughly, and as sure as *you* do, it will come home and blast your life, as it has blasted mine and the lives of those near and dear to me — and as it has invariably blasted the lives of all who have "tried it on".

Still that "if" stood in my way; however, I finally concluded to defer my journey home for a day or two, that I might have time to consider this new phase in the posture of affairs.

CHAPTER VIII.

BANK OF ENGLAND'S ARGUS EYES.

I again resume the thread of my narrative. It had occupied about two months in making the preparations described in the last chapter, and I was still so doubtful as to the possibility that the Bank of England would not discover the fraud with the first batch of bills, that I had fully prepared only what represented £4,250. I had preserved the endorsement blocks used in their manufacture, so that in case we were disappointed, and the bank really discounted them, we could rush up a larger number in a few days. It was exactly this doubt which had prevented the accumulation of a sufficient quantity of false bills; for despite the fair look of the thing, it was difficult to believe otherwise than that the bank had what looked like a vulnerable point guarded in some way that had escaped my scrutiny. Besides, I had the Warren account with the Bank of England, and the Horton account at the Continental Bank. With these simple means I now proposed to enter the bomb-proof vaults of the greatest financial fortress of which history gives account.

My brother was safely out of England. All was prepared for the trial test.

"Will the false bills go through? Will the argus eyes of the renowned Bank of England detect the imposture at the first glance?" These and similar questions agitated my mind at this juncture. To settle the question, I took the

£4,250 in false bills and went to Birmingham. There I engaged a room at the Queen's Hotel, and on paper brought with me I wrote in Warren's name, imitating his handwriting, to Mr. Francis, Manager of the Western Branch of the Bank of England, the following:

BIRMINGHAM, January 21, 1873.
DEAR SIR:
I hand you herewith, as per enclosed memorandum, bills for discount, the proceeds of which please place to my credit on receipt. I remain, dear sir, Yours very truly,
F. A. WARREN.

On the previous day all the money, except about one hundred pounds, had been drawn out of the London banks, so that in case of a discovery that would be the only additional loss — the previous preparations having cost about as much more. We had also prepared everything for an immediate flight in case it should prove a failure. I waited in Birmingham until the next day, in order to hear from Mr. Francis, or otherwise get a clue as to the fate of the false bills. In case the forgery had been discovered, he would doubtless reply to the letter all the same, and simultaneously put the Birmingham police on the scent, or send a detective from London to watch at the post-office and arrest the person who called for the letter. Suppose I should be thus arrested? Mr. Francis could not recognize me as otherwise connected with his customer, Warren, he never having seen me; but I should have been asked some awkward questions, and why I had called for Warren's letters. That I might have even a lame excuse ready, I wrote a note as follows:

BIRMINGHAM, January 22, 1873.
POSTMASTER:
SIR, — Please deliver any letters for me to the bearer, and oblige F. A. WARREN.

Calling at the post-office, and seeing no sign that it was specially watched, I handed in the order, and was given a letter. Had I been arrested, I should have said that I met a gentleman on the train and fell into conversation with him, and just before arriving at Birmingham he remarked that he must continue his journey to Liverpool, and would feel obliged to me if I would call for his letters and forward them. I hurried to catch the London train, and as soon as I was under way I opened the letter, which was to the following purport:

WESTERN BRANCH OF THE BANK OF ENGLAND,
LONDON, January 22, 1873.

F. A. WARREN, ESQ., P. O. Birmingham:

DEAR SIR, — Your favor of the 21st, enclosing £4,250 in bills for discount, is received, and proceeds of same passed to your credit as requested. Hoping you are recovering from the effects of the fall from your horse, and that I may have the pleasure of seeing you in London soon, I remain, dear sir,

Yours faithfully, P. M. FRANCIS.

On arrival in London, I gave Noyes "Warren" checks for £4,000, which he deposited in the Continental Bank to Horton's credit. I next filled in and signed Horton checks for about £3,000, with which he purchased United States bonds from Jay Cooke, M'Culloch & Co., at their banking-house in Lombard Street — the Wall Street of London.

This completed the operation, and as soon as we could prepare more false bills we were ready for another of exactly the same kind, only on a larger scale — and thus we kept repeating until the discovery.

Thinking that the purchase of such large sums of United States bonds from day to day might attract attention, I devised another plan, viz.: The forged bills being sent from Birmingham by mail, discounted and placed to Warren's credit at the Bank of England, the amount immediately transferred to the Horton account at the Continental Bank by means of Warren checks — I had Noyes reduce the latter account by drawing out Bank of England notes. These were taken to the bank and exchanged for gold, which was delivered in sealed bags of £1,000 each, and immediately carried back and exchanged for notes by another person. The object of this double exchange was to break the connection, it being obligatory that a list of the numbers of all notes paid out, and to whom, must be preserved by bankers and other dealers. Even when passed from hand to hand, the person who pays out a note must endorse on the back of it his or her name and address, and this notwithstanding that they are made payable "to bearer" exactly like "greenbacks." And, indeed, the disposal of so much gold without attracting notice was one of my chief anxieties — in fact, I found there was such a thing as having too much of that useful metal. The reader may realize this fact when I state that while the "business" was in operation our "income" was at times more than $50,000 per day.

I cannot refrain from relating, right here, an incident which illustrates the folly of "crowing before one is out of the woods," or "counting chickens before they are hatched."

One evening in January, while the "fraud machine" was in full operation, three stylishly dressed young men met in a private parlor of the St. James Hotel, Piccadilly. Two of them appeared to be in high spirits — perhaps possessed by evil spirits, whom spirits of another kind might conciliate — and one of the party called for a bottle of "Vueve Cliquot" in honor of the occasion, the "golden calf" having been worshiped that day to the jingle of many bags of sovereigns. The elder of the trio was in a pensive mood, and was rallied by his hilarious companions for his taciturnity, which became more marked as their merriment increased. They saw themselves safely back in America, the possessors of fortunes, however wrongfully obtained, yet obtained in a way that would leave behind no ruined widows and orphans to linger out the remainder of their blighted lives in poverty. That was a point which added zest to their enjoyment of the prospect. Being obtained from an institution, into whose impregnable vaults flowed the wealth of the world, was a source of inexpressible satisfaction to those gentlemanly appearing robbers. At last the elder could endure the situation no longer, and addressed the party very much as follows:

"Well, my friends, you believe that nothing can happen to hinder the full realization of your hopes, and that you are as safe as if you were already off for America; but I advise you to moderate your ardor and not be too sanguine — too certain. It is true that everything is so arranged, works so smoothly, and ourselves shrouded in so dense a fog — a London fog — of mystery, that, even in case of a premature discovery, they may not be able to reach us or get a clue to our personality.

"It appears as if the bank managers had heaped a mountain of gold out in the street, and had put up a notice, 'Please do not touch this,' and then had left it unguarded with the guileless confidingness of an Arcadian. Who could ever have imagined they would have left such an open path to their bags of gold? Thousands of Englishmen have gone out to India to 'shake the Banyan tree,' but this beats that 'legal' way of 'making' a fortune out of sight. Despite the smooth surface, I have a foreboding that Aeolus is brooding a storm that may send our gold-laden bark among the rocks, and ourselves with it. Negligence or accident will beat the 'best laid plans,' and we shall have the greatest success or the most terrible disaster possible. Let us do no more crowing until we are out of the woods."

With these words the speaker relapsed into his thoughtful mood, and soon after departed, leaving his goblet of Vueve Cliquot untasted.

It was not long after this that a truly laughable incident occurred. During our stay in London, it was frequently remarked that McDonald bore a strong general resemblance to the Prince of Wales. One afternoon Mac and I were sauntering past the "Horse-Guards," and as soon as the magnificent sentry (placed on horseback in the gateway) saw us, he brought his sword to the salute and kept it there until we were past. Exactly who he took *me* for has ever since been —not a *casus belli*—but a subject of curious cogitations—especially when in prison, writing petitions to the Home Office for my release — whether I should not refer the secretary of State to the sentry, in order to prove satisfactorily that I was a " somebody."

On the 27th day of February my associate and myself had a consultation as to whether we should stop with what we had, or put in one more batch of bills. It was finally decided to put in another, and the very last lot. In thus taking the pitcher once too often to the well, too little account was taken of two all-important points—neglect of business and the possibility of accidents, the latter, of course, usually arising out of the former. Early the next day I posted in Birmingham to the Bank more than $100,000 in false bills, congratulating myself that the affair was so nearly finished, and that the next day I should be off for America. When these bills were mailed the balance in both banks had been reduced to less than a thousand pounds.

Remaining in Birmingham, early the next morning I sent a cabman to the post-office with an order for letters addressed to Warren, and kept a watch on him to see if he was followed from the office. After satisfying myself that he was not being " shadowed," I got from him the letter, which was from Mr. Francis, stating that the bills had been received, discounted, and the proceeds placed to the credit of the Warren account. Of course, this was the last of a number of letters from Mr. Francis, which had been received by me during the progress of the affair, and as each came to hand I could not repress a feeling of regret that by the irony of fate I seemed destined, in the execution of " speculations," to abuse the confidence of some of the best of men. The fact that, as in the present instance, I was taking no advantage of facilities afforded by a position of trust—Mr. Francis never having seen me—was the excuse with which I had always, in such cases, tried to salve my conscience.

The letter in question satisfied me that our false bills had gone through the mill, and would be laid away in the vaults of the bank to be forgotten until they should become due two months later; and thus it would have been, but for an unforeseen occurrence to be related shortly. I hurried to the station, and taking a train arrived in London by the

GARRAWAY'S.

time the banks were open for business. In order to be certain that all was right before sending Noyes into the Continental Bank, I gave him a check for a small amount, which he sent in by a commissioner for collection, with order to bring the money to him at the Cannon Street Hotel. I took care to be in the bank when he arrived, that I might see what passed. The check was paid without demur, and he left the bank, I keeping him in view until he had passed the public house where Noyes was waiting for me. I hastened in and told him to go and get the money from the commissioner, which he did, then come to meet me at Garraway's, our usual place of rendezvous. Inasmuch as many generations of all nations visiting London, have been accustomed to resort to Garraway's coffee-house, for pleasure or business purposes, and as it was closed for the last time on Saturday, August 11, 1876, a picture of this celebrated place may be of interest to the reader.

At the time of the "South-Sea bubble," Dean Swift wrote the following lines regarding the brokers and their victims, the speculators, who were accustomed to congregate at Garraway's :

>There is a gulf where thousands fell,
>Here all the bold adventurers came,
>A narrow sound, though deep as hell—
>Change-alley is the dreadful name.

>Subscribers here by thousands float,
>And jostle one another down,
>Each paddling in his leaky boat,
>And here they fish for gold and drown.

>* * * *

>Meantime, secure on Garway cliffs,
>A savage race, by shipwrecks fed,
>Lie waiting for the founder'd skiffs,
>And strip the bodies of the dead.

Dr. Radcliffe, a celebrated character, was a rash speculator in the South-Sea scheme, and could always be found during business hours planted at a table, to watch the turns of the share market, and to receive his patients, as was the custom in the last century with coffee-houses in general. One day he had invested five thousand guineas in one project, and upon being informed that he had lost it all, replied:

"Why, 'tis but going up five thousand pairs of stairs more."
"This answer," says Sydney Smith, "deserves a statue."

Coming down to later times, we find in Dickens's "Pickwick Club," where Sergeant Buzfuz, in the case of Bardell *vs.* Pickwick, quotes the following letter:

GARRAWAY'S, twelve o'clock.

DEAR MRS. B.: — Chops and tomato sauce.

Yours,   PICKWICK.

As some of my readers may be in a Pickwickian state of mind on the food question, I will reserve the account of the discovery of the great fraud, and the arrest of Noyes, for the next chapter.

Chapter IX.

THE FRAUD DISCOVERED — NOYES ARRESTED — A CLEARANCE — AN IMPORTANT PIECE OF BLOTTING PAPER — FLIGHT OF MCDONALD — EXAMINATION OF NOYES AT THE MANSION HOUSE BEFORE LORD MAYOR WATERLOW — THE BANK SOLICITOR, C. K. FRESHFIELD, M. P. — DR. KENEALY.

IT appears that when the last lot of bills arrived from Birmingham they were handed by the manager, as usual, to a clerk whose duty it was to look over and enter them in the books. In running them over, he threw out two on which the date of the acceptance had not been put. Supposing this to have been an oversight of the acceptors, no notice was taken of the irregularity beyond laying the bills aside, that the supposed neglect might be rectified. Accordingly, on the morning of the 1st of March, 1873, the bills were sent to B. W. Blydenstein (the supposed acceptor), and were at once declared to be forgeries. Instant measures were taken to arrest the perpetrators. This occurred just after we had sent the commissioner with a Horton check as related in the last chapter.

Upon meeting Noyes at Garraway's I gave him Warren checks for seventy-five thousand dollars, with which he purchased United States bonds from Messrs. Jay Cooke & Co. I also gave him about thirty thousand dollars in Warren checks to deposit to the credit of the Horton account. After having accomplished that business, it only remained for him to withdraw the money from the Horton account, which would finish, and we be ready to leave the country with our booty.

A quarter of an hour would end my anxieties!

It had been my intention to send a commissioner to draw the money, so that in the apparently impossible case of a discovery Noyes would be safe from arrest. Should there be a premature "tumble" and we become aware of it in time, we could easily get him out of the country — he being the only one who was known to the bankers. But having just visited Jay Cooke & Co. and the Continental Bank, he justly felt certain that all was right, and thought it would be best, and quite safe, for him to go and do the business in person instead of sending a commissioner.

We had previously sent commissioners for large sums in bonds, etc.; but in such cases they had acted only as messengers, not knowing the value of the packages they carried. The checks we had sent by them were for small sums, and now to send one to draw $30,000 might cause inquiry at the Continental Bank. For these reasons I concluded to let Noyes have his own way. Had I known what was at that moment passing not a stone's throw from where we sat in Garraway's, my thoughts would have been of quite a different nature. After the discovery, as related, the telegraph was set to work, and detectives procured from the Bow Street police station, which was but a short distance from where we sat discussing our next and last move — the last indeed! They went to the Continental, Horton's bank, and waited to meet Noyes as he came in about one o'clock P. M. to draw the money. He was arrested and taken to Bow Street station, the party passing close by me on the way, of course neither Noyes or I taking any notice of each other. As I had foreseen and provided for this possible contingency, the occurrence did not alarm me, for I knew that *if all my precautions had been lived up to,* no harm beyond temporary inconvenience could come to Noyes, and not the slightest clue be obtained to connect Mac or myself with the fraud. Austin, the only other one known to the bankers, was, as I supposed, safe in the United States; therefore, as I felt secure that no information would be got out of Noyes, all we had to do was to lie quietly in London until the furore of excitement was a little cooled, and then to make our way out of the country at our

leisure. Nothwithstanding these seemingly impregnable plans and precautions, and as a striking example of how crime comes to light, it will be interesting to have the causes which nullified the execution of the ideas outlined in the last sentence.

During the operation Mac occupied lodgings in an aristocratic quarter, St. James Place, Piccadilly. There all the bills were made. When the last lot was ready, I made away with and destroyed by burning or otherwise, the articles used in their manufacture.

As soon as Noyes was arrested, I went to Mac's rooms and made a clearance. As I was about to put all the waste papers in the fire Mac said he had some letters to write and asked me to leave a piece of blotting paper. I selected a piece that appeared not to have been used and laid it aside for him — a fatal concession, as will be seen in the account of the trial, showing what telling use was made of it. I was less particular in the clearance because when I represented to him the danger of an American moving from his lodgings at such a juncture, he agreed to remain quietly there. Then judge of my astonishment later in the day, when he said to me at Garraway's: "Well, I've got all my things out of that place, anyway." It was too late to repair so false a step, and he assured me that he had not left a scrap of paper behind. Subsequent events showed that his landlady saw in a paper an account of the forgery and arrest of Noyes, and coupling it with her lodger's precipitate flight — he having previously given no notice of his intention to leave — her suspicions were aroused; she went directly to the rooms and gathered up every loose bit of paper she could find, among which the only thing that proved of special value was the piece of blotting paper, and sent word to the police station.

Mac paid the penalty of this thoughtless act as this piece of blotter proved to be the principal, if not the only direct link, which connected him with the forgery.

I had occasion to part from Mac for an hour, and on my

return at about six P. M., found a note written by him, stating that he had just time to catch the last evening train for Dover. He really went to Liverpool; but becoming suspicious, doubled on the police, ran to Chester, from there crossed the country by way of Taunton to Southampton, crossed to Havre, from which place he managed to get on board the steamship *Thuringia*, and sailed for New York.

MANSION HOUSE, ILLUMINATED.

This unexpected departure disconcerted my plans completely. The effect it had on my future proceedings will be detailed in the chapters relating to my flight through Ireland, and beyond.

CHAPTER X.

HUNTED THROUGH IRELAND — $2,500 REWARD FOR MY CAPTURE — DETECTIVES "SPOT" ME AT THE CORK RAILWAY STATION — OBLIGED TO ABANDON TAKING PASSAGE BY THE ILL-FATED ATLANTIC — A GAME OF "HARE AND HOUNDS" — ELUDING A DETECTIVE "TRAP" — ENGLISH MISRULE IN IRELAND — AM TAKEN FOR A PRIEST — A TYPOGRAPHICAL THUNDERBOLT AT LISMORE — AN EARLY MORNING WALK — A RIDE ON AN IRISH JAUNTING-CAR — "ON THE ROAD TO CLONMEL" — SHELTER IN A "SHEBEEN" — HOW THIRSTY SOULS GET THE "CRAYTHUR" IN IRELAND — A GOOD OLD IRISH LADY — PURSUIT, AND REFUGE IN A RUINED COTTAGE AT CAHIR.

WITHOUT the remotest suspicion that my right name was known, or that anything had been discovered to show my connection with the fraud, I resolved to take the steamer *Atlantic* of the White Star Line, at Queenstown, for New York. Knowing that all the railway stations in London were being watched, and that any man buying a ticket for America might have to give an account of himself, I sent a porter to purchase a ticket for Dublin *via* Holyhead. I intended taking the 9 P. M. mail train, and, as a precaution, I waited until the last moment, after the passengers were on board and the waiting-room doors shut. As the mail was being transferred from the wagons to the train, I took the opportunity to walk through the big gate unobserved amid the rush and confusion. The car doors were all locked, but on showing my ticket to a guard (conductor) he let me into a compartment, no doubt supposing that I had obtained admission to the station from the waiting-room and had been loitering about. The same was probably the case with the two or three other men looking out of the waiting-room window at the platform, whom I judged to be detectives. The train rolled out of the station, and soon I was leaving London behind at the rate of fifty miles an hour. After midnight we took the steamer at Holyhead and arrived at Dublin about seven A. M. I should not have felt so comfortable throughout this night's journey had I known that the telegraph was flashing in all directions :

"£500 reward for the capture of George Bidwell, who is supposed to be one of the persons engaged in the great bank forgery. He is an American, about forty years of age, of dark complexion, and is supposed to be in Ireland."

A whole column regarding myself and my transactions was published in the Dublin papers of that morning. Not suspecting they contained "news" regarding me, I neglected purchasing one, and remaining ignorant of my imminent danger, took the train for Cork, where I arrived about four P. M. I had two or three London papers of the previous day in my hand as I left the station. I had never been in Cork until then, and as I passed into the street two detectives, who were watching the passengers, turned and followed me. A few yards from the station one of them stepped up by my side and said :

"Have you ever been here before?"

I slightly turned my head toward him, gave a haughty glance as I replied, "Yes,"— then looked straight ahead and continued my slow gait, paying no further attention to him. He continued walking by my side for a few steps, as if irresolute, then dropped to the rear, rejoining his companion. I did not dare to look around, or make inquiry as to the location of the wharf from which the tug-boat started to convey mail and passengers to the New York steamers, which waited in the outer harbor. Therefore I continued my walk along what appeared to be the main business street, perhaps for a quarter of a mile, then turned into a druggist's and called for some Spanish licorice. This was done to enable me to ascertain if the detectives were still following. In a moment they passed the shop gazing intently in, and saw me leaning carelessly against the counter with my face partially turned to the street. As soon as I had paid for the licorice, I continued my walk in the same direction, but saw nothing of the men, they having evidently stopped in some place to let me get ahead once more. In a short time I approached an inclosure, over the gate of which was a sign that informed me I had come by accident direct to the wharf of the New York steamers. Entering I found the place crowded, and the tug-boat ready to convey the passengers to the steamer *Atlantic*. Before attempting to step aboard the tug I took a covert look around and saw my two detectives standing back in one corner with their eyes fixed upon me all but their heads being concealed behind the crowd waiting to see their friends off for America. Apparently unconscious of their presence, I threw my papers, one by one down among the passengers; and as the deck of the boat was eight or ten feet below, the detectives could not see to whom they were thrown. I stood leaning on the rail a short time gazing at the scene, then left the wharf not even glancing in the direction of the detectives. I felt that any attempt of mine to embark would precipitate their movements, therefore I at once abandoned all ideas of taking passage from Queenstown.

Now mark the irony of fate! That was the last passage ever made by the magnificent steamer *Atlantic!* Some magnetic influence deranged her compass so that she ran twenty miles out of her course, striking on the coast of Nova Scotia, at Meager's Head, Prospect Harbor, broke in two, then rolling into deep water, sank in a few minutes. Out of 1002 persons on board 560 perished, including most of the saloon passengers and all the women and children. The elegant cabins and state-rooms became their tombs — and one might have been mine. But not for me such favoring fate; a moment's struggle ended their sufferings, while I was left to undergo the pangs of a thousand deaths!

I continued my walk up a hill among the private residences of the city, and hailing a cab told the driver to take me back to the station. Eager for a job, he asked to drive me a mile beyond on the railway. Thinking I might elude the detectives at the Queenstown station, I acceded and he made his little Irish horse rush along at a pace which brought us to the stopping-place just before the train arrived.

I purchased a ticket and hastened into a carriage, where, lo and behold! sat the two detectives. A few minutes brought us to Cork again. I was not yet aware they were in possession of my right name and the knowledge that a reward of five hundred pounds was offered for my capture, nor that their hesitation was occasioned by doubts as to my identity, which the first false step on my part might remove. I did not suppose they were looking especially for me, but for any one in general whose actions and appearance might indicate that he was one of the operators in the bank forgery. Under this erroneous belief, I crossed to the Dublin station, which was a quarter of a mile from that of the Cork and Queenstown, to inquire for a dispatch that I expected from London to the name of Bodell. When I stepped up to the telegraph-counter and gave the name, the pretty girl in charge looked at me in a very "speaking" manner, and without making examination replied, "No." As I turned away, I saw my two detectives standing at the other side of the room. "Well," I thought to myself, "this is very strange; I left the Queenstown station ahead of them, and here they are again, all alive." I walked away into the most thronged streets of the business part of the city; turning a corner, I glanced backwards and saw them following at some distance in the rear. As soon as I had fairly turned the corner, I started at a fast walk, turning the next before they came in view; and after three or four such turnings I went into a small temperance hotel and took lodgings for the night. There was but a single commercial traveler in the sitting-room — a special room set apart in every English hotel, sacred to the "drummer" fraternity. In the course of the evening he handed me a small railway map of Ireland, which, in my subsequent flight through the country, proved of incalculable service to me.

The next morning I went out and purchased a hand-bag, a Scotch cap, and a cheap, frieze ulster. My night's cogitations had not enabled me to solve the detective problem, but I felt confident that *something* was decidedly wrong. I then hired a covered cab, driving past the post-office to reconnoiter, and saw one of the detectives standing in the door-way. This sight deterred me from going in to ask for a letter. Dismissing my cab, I took another and drove to the place where I had made my purchases, taking them into the cab, and going through a by-street which brought me close to my hotel.

From the commercial-room in the second floor front, I looked out and marked the farthest house I could see to the left, on the opposite side. Stepping to the desk, I wrote an order directing the postmaster to deliver any letters to my (Bodell's) address to the bearer. This I gave to a cabman, instructing him to drive to the post-office and bring my mail to the house I had marked, returning myself to the commercial-room to watch. In a few minutes I saw the cabman drive to the house, and seeing no one waiting there, he turned and drove slowly down the street past the hotel, holding up at arm's length a letter to attract my notice — which it did to my two detectives walking along a short distance behind him, on the hotel side of the street, with noses elevated and eyes peering everywhere.

"Well," I thought, "this is getting to be hot, and it is time for me to 'skip' Cork." I was now fully aroused to a sense of my danger. No one happening to be in the commercial-room for the moment, I left my hat on the sofa, and wearing the Scotch cap, slipped downstairs just as they were past the hotel, following them until I came to where the cab was waiting with my luggage. I ordered the driver to take me to a canal-boat wharf, where I dismissed him; then, with bag in hand, I walked across the canal bridge, stopped in a small shop and hired a smaller boy to go for a jaunting-car, and a few minutes later I was rolling to the northward.

On the road I threw some small coins to poor-looking

people, who then, as now, comprised among their numbers the most honest patriots and the truest-hearted sons of Erin. While gazing upon the mud huts and turf cottages which constituted, with but few exceptions, the abiding-places of a poverty-stricken people, I could not help apostrophizing thus: " To what a state of degradation has not English misrule and oppression, long continued, brought the noble Celtic race? Doubtless over this very road many a humble Irish peasant has been hunted to the death at a time when it was only necessary for his English murderer to offer in defense, before a jury composed of his own countrymen, that he had only killed an Irishman; where life was no more valued by the English of that time than are now the lives of the convicts in the English prisons." How low that valuation is may be judged by the words spoken to me by the chief warder of Dartmoor prison, in 1877: " We think no more of killing a convict than we do of killing a dog; indeed, we value the life of a good dog above that of a convict."

Seeing me throwing the pence to the poor folk, cabby took it into his head that I must be a priest — a good criterion of the estimation in which the benevolence of the Fathers is held by their own people. And I may here remark that all the Catholic priests I have known, occupying the post of chaplain to the convicts of that religion, were without exception faithful and entirely devoted to the duties of their holy calling, speaking fearlessly to the authorities whenever Catholic prisoners were being wrongly treated by the warders. I had no intention of traveling as a priest, and when I told the driver as much he would not believe it, but insisted that I was really a priest traveling incognito; therefore, when we stopped at a small, wayside tavern, about twelve miles from Cork and two to Fermoy, he privately informed the mistress that I was a priest who did not want the fact to become known. Accordingly the good woman treated me with marked attention during my short stay. It was then nearly sunset, and as I did not wish the cabman to get back to Cork until late at night, I kept him eating and drinking until dark, when I paid the bill and started him homeward, uproariously rejoicing. I then started for Fermoy station, about two miles distant, taking the hostler along to carry my bag. When within half a mile of the village I let him return. While passing through the village I went into a shop and purchased a different Scotch cap, the " Glengary."

Arriving at the station, I noticed a man near the ticket-office who appeared to be watching those who were purchasing tickets. This made me change my plan — instead of taking a ticket to Dublin, I bought one for Lismore, the end of the road in the opposite direction. The exclamation, " Well, are you going to stay all night?" was the first intimation I had of our arrival at that place. I rubbed my sleepy eyes, and saw with dismay that all the passengers were gone, and one of the porters was putting out the lights. At the platform I found a cab, and by nine P. M. I was at the Lismore House.

After eating supper I entered the sitting-room, finding a single occupant whom I took to be a lawyer; and, judging by his conversation and manner, in the light of later events, I do not doubt that he surmised who I was. He was reading a newspaper, which he once or twice offered to me; but not dreaming of the interesting nature of its contents, I declined to take it from him. About ten P. M. the gentleman retired, leaving his paper on the table. I carelessly picked it up, and the first thing that caught my eyes was a displayed heading in large type:

500 pounds reward for the capture of George Bidwell, who is in Ireland. He cannot escape, for all the stations are watched and the seaports guarded. The whole constabulary and detective force of the country are after him (etc.)

A thunderbolt, indeed! For a few minutes I stared at the paper in blank dismay. It was fortunate for my temporary safety that there were no witnesses present. " Well," I thought to myself, " this *is* a predicament! How did they obtain my right name? I thought I had covered up the whole affair so deep in mystery that not a clue to our personality could be obtained; and here in this paper appears the whole business as correctly as if I had told them myself! There has been carelessness or treachery somewhere!"

I sat for an hour alone in this Lismore Hotel, utterly dumbfounded, bewildered, paralyzed. I had experienced some shocks, some "take-downs," in my time, but never one to compare with this. After priding myself in having laid a plan and managed an operation to lighten the plethoric money-bags of the most gigantic financial institution in all the world — one that never has less than $60,000,000 in its impregnable vaults — an institution which boasted that its system of transacting business had become so perfect that it was secure from the attempts of the designing, yet had permitted me and my assistants to carry off its bags of gold *ad libitum*, — here I was in such a fix, and everything supposed to have been so carefully hidden, so deeply buried, that nothing less than superhuman genius could unearth it, had come to the surface as by the touch of a magic wand in the hands of a prestidigitateur.

Arousing myself from a state of mental stupefaction hitherto unknown, I began to realize the necessity of immediate action if I wished to avoid falling into the merciless jaws of the British Lion. I put the paper into the fire, and retired to the room allotted to me. For the first time I fully realized how far I had departed from the principles inculcated by my father and mother. For the first time I saw myself on the verge of the yawning gulf toward which I had been almost imperceptibly gliding ever since the day of my fatal meeting with Frank Kibbe in Baltimore.

Before daylight in the morning I had decided upon the first step, and as the lawyer had asked me if I intended to remain over Sunday, I resolved to be as far away as possible before he was out of bed. While it was yet dark in the house, I left my bag in the bedroom and crept gently down the stairs to the basement, where the porter-hostler was sleeping in a box of rags. I suppose the poor wretch had not long finished his multifarious duties, for 1 could arouse him only to a state of semi-consciousness, and could get no information from him. I then went up to the front door, carefully turned the key and stepped out on the piazza which, ran along the front of the hotel. Another shock was in store for me. A man posted on the other side of the street was watching the hotel!

It was now quite light, and I sauntered carelessly up the street, apparently taking no notice of the man over the way, and endeavoring to show by my actions that 1 was out for an airing before breakfast.

As I turned the next corner and glanced back, I saw him following. I noticed a place where jaunting-cars were to be let, but passed on, at each turn glancing back to see my follower the same distance in the rear. I now took a circuit around by the hotel, but instead of going in, I hastened and turned the next corner beyond— he, when reaching the corner near the hotel, not seeing me, doubtless thought I had gone in, and planted himself in his old position. I thought Lismore to be getting rather hot, and hastening to the livery stable, found the hostler just getting up. He informed me that all the horses were engaged for the day (Sunday, March 9, 1873) except one, the fastest they had, but as this was engaged for a long journey on Tuesday, they were letting him have a rest. I said: "But, my good' fellow, I must have a horse, and at once, with you to drive, and there will be a half sovereign for a good Irishman, such as I see before me." My "blarney" began to do its work. Scratching his head, he finally said: "Well, I will waken up my master, and you can talk with him." So he rapped at a window, and soon a night-capped head appeared, and after some parley the master consented to let me his equipage. In a few minutes from the time I had lost sight of my follower we were rattling out of the town of Lismore at the full speed of a blooded Irish horse. I had left my bag behind, taking only the Scotch caps and ulster with me from the hotel. I found, by reference to the small map and railway guide, that Clonmel was less than thirty miles distant, and connected with Dublin by a branch line. When I engaged the jaunting-car, I had told the owner that it was uncertain what part of the day I should require it, and after we were about five miles from Lismore I said to the driver:

"You say that you are going to Clonmel on Tuesday for a passenger. Well, now, as I must go there before I leave this part of the country, you may as well continue in that direction, and I can return with you on Tuesday."

This pleased him, and we drove on till about noon, when we stopped at a country grocery about five miles from Clonmel. As we drove up to the door, the words of an old Irish song went jingling through my brain:

"At the sign of the bell,
    On the road to Clonmel,
        Pat Flagherty kept a neat shebeen."

The rain poured down in torrents. I gave my driver a lunch of bread and cheese, which — of course there — included whisky. I also gave him a sovereign, telling him to pay his master for the horse-hire and keep the change for himself; then started him back brim full of delight and the "craythur," receiving his parting salute:

"Yer 'onor is a jintleman, and no mistake."

I arranged with the store-keeper to let a boy take me in his car to Clonmel.

"The Green Isle!" Well, I found out that day what keeps the grass green in Ireland. My Irish frieze and every thread on me were water-logged, yet the Irish lad, my driver, took the "buckets-full" as a matter of course. Amidst this deluge of rain, we arrived in Clonmel and stopped at a "shebeen," kept by the boy's uncle — driving into the back yard through a gate in a board-fence fifteen feet high, which shut it in from the street.

I went into a room in the rear of the sale-room, the door

of which stood open so that I could see all that passed within; and, as I stood drying my clothes by the turf fire, I saw how thirsty souls on the " ould sod," evaded the Sunday liquor law. The proprietor stood in the shop in a position whence he could covertly keep an eye on the policeman patrolling the street, and as soon as he was out of sight, a signal was given, the back-yard gate thrown open, when a dozen men rushed in, and the gate closed. Coming hilariously through the dwelling into the shop, these were soon busily drinking their " potheen," laughing and boasting about how cunningly they had " done the cowardly informer of a policeman."

It was now two o'clock P. M.; the rain had ceased, and starting out, I walked along a main street until I saw a sign, " Cabs to let." I went into the house and was shown into an inner room, where the proprietress sat crooning over a turf fire. She motioned me to a seat beside her, and when I told her I wished for a conveyance to take me to Cahir, a place eight miles distant, she asked me several questions, among others, how long I wished to be gone, and if I were not an American. To all of which, I replied to the following effect: That I was going to visit some friends who were officers stationed in the fort at Cahir; and as to her mistaking me for an American, the ancestors of the " Yankees " went from about Norfolk county, England, to America, of course taking the accent with them, and I being from the former place (Norfolk) of course had the same accent.

This explanation appeared to satisfy the old lady, and she became quite confidential; and, anxious to remove from my mind any trace of offense at her unusual questioning, she drew closer to me and said:

" I can see that you are all right; but, the fact is, that the captain of police sent an order that I should notify him at once, in case any stranger wished to hire a vehicle, especially if I thought him an American. But I do not care for the curs; they are nothing but a parcel of spies and informers in the pay of the English government; so even if you were the one they are looking for, they will wait a long time for me to inform them, and you shall have my best horse and a good driver."

I heartily thanked the good old Irish lady — for I have found true ladies and gentlemen among the poor and humble as well as the wealthy, especially in Ireland — and in a few minutes I was bowling gaily along toward Cahir.

This is a small, ancient, walled garrison town, the nearest railway station being at Clonmel. This miniature city has been the scene of many a heart-stirring event in the distant past. Here Cromwell was for a time held at bay, and his fanatical hordes made their Celtic opponents pay in blood for their patriotic and desperate defense of their homes and firesides.

Driving through the town gate, I saw in the main street a grocery store with a blind down, and telling the driver to halt there, I paid him and sent him back. I then went into the grocery, and after taking a lunch of bread and cheese, continued my walk up the street. I saw a hotel just ahead, but not wishing to attract attention to my movements, I crossed to the opposite side, and while doing so, glanced back and saw a car come through the same town gate I had just entered, and dash furiously up the street, pulling up at the walk a few yards behind me. Just as they sprang out, I turned to the left into a narrow lane in which I saw a gateway to the fort, just within the entrance of which a sentry was pacing, there being opposite several roofless cottages. The soldier's back being turned, quick as thought I sprang unseen within one of these, and in a moment I heard some men run around the corner and interrogate the soldier, who stoutly declared that no one had entered. The men then demanded to see the captain, were admitted, and after a short time I heard them come out and depart. I stood in that ruin two mortal hours until dusk, then walked out unseen by the sentry, and turning to the left, came into a narrow street lined with small dwelling houses.

Chapter XI.

AN UNCEREMONIOUS CALL — "I AM A FENIAN LEADER" — A "STORY" TOLD IN THE DARK — MALOY HELPS MY ESCAPE ON AN IRISH JAUNTING-CAR — EGGS — A POLICEMAN ANXIOUS TO OBTAIN THE FIVE HUNDRED POUNDS REWARD — DUBLIN AGAIN — A JEWESS'S BLESSING — I TURN RUSSIAN, AND LATER BECOME A FRENCHMAN — BELFAST DETECTIVES — ESCAPE INTO SCOTLAND — THE OTHER SIDE OF THE STORY — A BOW-STREET DETECTIVE'S ADVENTURES WHILE HUNTING ME THROUGH IRELAND — CROSS-QUESTIONING MY JAUNTING-CAR DRIVER — A "COLD WATER CURE" — HOT ON THE TRAIL — NOT IN THE FORT — A FRUITLESS HUNT — MANY INNOCENTS ARRESTED — MALOY BECOMES A "KNOW-NOTHING."

CROSSING the narrow street in Cahir, referred to at the close of the last chapter, I went in hap-hazard at the first door, without knocking, and saw a family eating their humble supper. As I walked in I addressed the family at the table thus:

"Good evening. Pardon my intrusion, and do not disturb yourselves; but by all means finish your supper."

"Good evening, sir," was the reply from the man, whom I will call Maloy. "We are glad to see you; will you sit by and have pot-luck with us?"

"No, thank you," I answered. "I am an American — and it is my custom when traveling in any country to make unceremonious calls like this, in order to see the people as they really are at home."

After supper was over I related to Maloy and his family several stories and incidents concerning the Fenians and their doings in America, which of course interested them greatly. When it was fairly dark I arose to go, and Maloy went outside with me. He had previously informed me that he was employed by the government in the civil service I will not state in what capacity, for although so many years have elapsed, the true-hearted Irishman may still be earning his bread in the same humble employment, and the knowledge that he assisted one whom he supposed to be a Fenian leader in 1873 might even now cost him dearly. If what he did was discovered at the time, and he suffered in consequence — should he be still alive, or if not, his wife or children — it would give me great pleasure to hear from the family, and to render them such aid as is now in my power. I am sure they cannot have forgotten me. When we were outside the door I said:

"The fact is, Maloy, I am a Fenian leader, and the police are after me! I have been dodging them for two days, and they are looking for me now in Cahir! I have important papers for prominent Fenians in various parts of Ireland, and it would delay our plans if I am obliged to destroy them. But I fear I must do so at once, unless you can help me. I would almost sooner forfeit my life than to lose these papers, and I shall fight to my last breath rather than let them fall into the hands of the police, for it might be the ruin of several good men! My plan is to double back to Clonmel, and I want your assistance to get me out of Cahir!"

"O, sir," he replied "it is too bad you did not let me know a little sooner, for the mail-car is gone; it starts at six o'clock."

Just as he finished speaking, a car came rumbling past, and he exclaimed joyfully:

"We are in luck! There goes the mail-car to the post-office! Come with me!"

We hastened through a narrow, dark lane to the gate — the same I had entered from Clonmel — walked through and at a hundred yards beyond waited for the mail-car, which soon came along. Maloy being well acquainted with the driver, hailed him, saying that a friend of his wanted a ride to Clonmel.

After shaking hands warmly with Maloy, I climbed upon the car, and the next instant I was whirling along — into fresh dangers — in that unique vehicle, an Irish jaunting-car.

Arriving near Clonmel I saw a tavern, and ascertaining from the driver that it was near the railway station, I left the car and entered the place, only to find that the best, and in fact the sole food to be had for supper was eggs. Having been on the move since dawn, after a sleepless night, and almost without food, I hesitate to divulge how many eggs I disposed of that evening, for the statement might tend to throw distrust on the general veracity of my narrative. Having dried my wet clothes and put myself into a presentable condition, I went to the railway station to take the eleven P. M. train to Dublin. Seating myself on a bench outside, I handed some money to a porter and sent him for a ticket, which he obtained. There were but a few waiting about, so I stepped into the small waiting-room and sat down near three other men. The one nearest, whom I at once put down for a local policeman in private clothes, turned and spoke to me. I replied with civility to his questions until finally he said: "But, are you not an American?" I replied to his startling question in such a manner that he appeared satisfied.

"You must excuse me, sir, for questioning you," he explained, "but there has been a great forgery in London, and it is said some of the parties are in Ireland, and I am anxious to get a claim on the 500 pounds that is offered for each one of them." I told him that instead of being offended, I was greatly pleased to see the zeal he exhibited in the execution of his duties, and expressed the hope that he might be successful in securing at least one of the forgers, which would give him not only the 500 pounds, but undoubtedly promotion. I got on the train all right, resolving that I would not speak another word of English while in Ireland, and forthwith turned into a Russian, who could speak ".une veree leetel Froncais," confident that I should not be in danger of exposure by encounter with any one who could speak the Russian language. I threw away the ordinary Scotch cap I had been wearing, and put on the Glengary. When I arrived at the Maryborough junction, the train on the main line from Cork was late, and I walked up and down on the platform, well-knowing that the detectives would scrutinize more closely those who appeared to shrink from observation; therefore I affected the bearing of a Russian prince as nearly as I knew how.

I got on the train unmolested, and arrived in Dublin at one A. M.

There appeared to be some special watching of those leaving the train, but I passed out unchallenged and took a cab. Not knowing the name of any hotel, I told the driver I would direct the route as we passed along, and he drove away at a great pace. Very soon I noticed another cab following at an equal speed. I had mine turn a corner, but the one behind came thundering after; and though I bade my driver to turn at nearly every corner, still I could not shake off my supposed pursuer until, after apparently being followed about two miles, the stern-chaser turned off in another direction, much to my relief. We soon approached the Cathedral Hotel, where I alighted about two A. M., rang up the porter, and was shown to a room.

At seven o'clock in the morning I sent for my bill, left the hotel, went direct to the "Jew" quarter, and purchased a valise and some second-hand clothes. Noticing the old Jewess's looks of curiosity at seeing one of my appearance making such purchases, I remarked: "A Fenian friend has got himself into a scrape, and the police are after him; so I am going to get him out of the country, and wish to let him have some things that do not have too new a look." At hearing those (in Ireland) magic words, "Fenian," "police," she became all smiles, let me fill the valise with old garments at my own price, and at parting said: "God bless you! May you have good luck, and get him off safe to America!"

I then went to a more pretentious locality, where I procured a silk hat draped with mourning crape, put the Glengary in my pocket, and became a Frenchman. At this moment I discovered that I had left in my room at the hotel a large silk neck-wrapper on which were embroidered the initials "G. B." I immediately stepped into a shop and left my new purchases, resuming the Scotch cap, and started for the hotel (where I had given no name) to secure the dangerous article left behind. Coming in sight of the hotel, I saw a man stationed opposite, leaning on a cane, who appeared to be watching the house. As I approached nearer he kept his eyes covertly fixed upon me; therefore, instead of entering the hotel, I walked past it and turned the next corner, glancing backward as I did so, and, to my dismay, saw the man following me. I now adopted the same plan of action that succeeded so well at Cork, and in a half-hour I had shaken him off and returned to the place where I had left my new silk hat and valise. Donning the hat, with valise in hand, I was soon seated in an Irish jaunting-car, on my way to a station about ten miles out on the railway to Belfast.

Upon reflection, I was satisfied that the chambermaid had found the silk wrapper and taken it to the hotel office. There the initials, together with the knowledge of my arrival at so unusual an hour, without baggage, and my early departure, had aroused the suspicion that I was the George Bidwell of the newspapers, and the police had been notified at once. At about eleven A. M. I arrived at the station, and going into a store, paid my Dublin cabman, and called for a lunch. About five minutes before the train was due from Dublin, I walked into the empty station, presented myself at the ticket-office, and said, "Parlez vous Français, Monsieur?" and received the reply, "No." I then said, in a mongrel of French and English, that I wished for a ticket to Drogheda — not daring to purchase one through to Belfast. Supposing me to be a French gentleman, he was very polite and ordered the porter to take my baggage to the platform. There I found myself the solitary waiting passenger. As the train approached, I saw a pair of heads projecting from the carriage windows, eagerly scanning the platform. Two men jumped off, and hastening to the station-master, began to talk to him in an excited manner, all the time glancing toward me. As I passed near the group to get on the train, I heard the agent say: "He is a Frenchman." No doubt he informed them that I had purchased a ticket to a way-station only — a fact that would naturally allay suspicion. At the next stopping-place they actually arrested a man, but went no further.

I afterward ascertained that twelve men were arrested on that and the preceding day, among the number being a fraudulent debtor trying to escape to America by the same steamer — the *Atlantic*.

The following extracts from contemporary newspapers will give the reader some idea as to what a "hot" place Ireland was for me:

[By cable to the New York *Herald*.]

LONDON, March 18, 1873.

Three shabbily dressed men, who from their accent are believed to be Americans, were arrested in Cork, Ireland, this morning, while attempting to deposit $12,000 in that city.

They are supposed to be the parties who recently committed the frauds on the Bank of England.

[From the London *Times* of same date.]

TO EDITOR OF "TIMES":

SIR, — The case of Dr. Hessel has been so lately before the public, and so much has been written both in the English and German papers against the English police, that probably a little evidence upon the procedure of the German (or, I ought probably to say, the Bavarian) may not be uninteresting at the present moment. Myself and son, a sub-lieutenant, R. N., made a great effort to reach the grotesque old city of Nuremburg on Saturday last, 8th March, arriving there about seven P. M. We were asked to put our names in the stranger's book, as usual, which we did, and retired to bed. Imagine our surprise, on rising on Sunday morning, at receiving a visit from one of the chief police officers requesting us to "legitimize ourselves." I asked him his object for making this demand, when he replied that a man named "Horton" was wanted by the English police.

In vain I showed him an old passport and letters addressed to me, showing that my name was Hutton; he informed me that I could not leave my room, and placed two policemen at the door. At one o'clock I remembered an influential inhabitant of the town who knew me, and I sent for him. He at once went to headquarters and gave bond for me to a large amount, and at six o'clock in the evening myself and son were released. You will remember that in the case of Dr. Hessel four persons swore to his identity before he was deprived of his liberty. In my case a similar name to that required was sufficient to deprive me of mine.

I have since received, thanks to the strenuous and prompt action of the British Minister at Munich, a very ample apology in writing for the blunder that had been committed. It is signed by the Burgermeister of the city, and as the intelligence of this worthy seems to be equaled by his simplicity, he sends me a safe pass to protect me in my further travels, in case Hutton should again be considered the same as Horton. I remain, sir,

Your obedient servant,

CHAS. W. C. HUTTON,

Ex-Sheriff, London and Middlesex.

FRANKFORT-ON-THE-MAINE, March 15, 1873.

I now return to my narrative. In the second-class compartment where I sat were two burly, loud-talking, well-informed farm proprietors, one of whom had imbibed a little too freely of the native distillation. The sober one had just finished reading a column article on the "Great Bank Forgery" to his lively companion, who at length turned and addressed me. I answered him politely in broken French, and he then went on to give his opinion of the bank affair, as nearly as I can remember, as follows:

"You, being a Frenchman, don't understand about our great bank; but I tell you those Yankees did a mighty thing when they attacked that powerful institution. The one they have got penned up here in Ireland can't possibly escape; indeed, according to the newspapers, he is already in the hands of the police. I am almost sorry to hear it, for in getting the best of that bank so cleverly the rascal deserves to get off; and see, here is a description of him."

I looked at the paper and saw that it was a fair general outline of my appearance, even to my ulster which I had with me in the valise, and the Scotch cap which was in my pocket. Before we reached Drogheda I had explained to one of my new friends, in broken French, that, owing to my ignorance of the English language, I had purchased a wrong ticket, and being liable to make a similar mistake, should feel obliged if he would take the trouble to procure me a ticket at that station. He readily assented, and by this means I procured it without exposing myself. The hunt for me was becoming so extremely hot that I dared not show myself again at a ticket-office; and if I should be found on a train ticketless, that fact might lead to closer scrutiny — the rule in that country being that every passenger must be provided with a ticket before entering a car, under the penalty of fine or imprisonment.

The train arrived in Belfast at nine P. M., and I at once took a cab to the Glasgow steamer. It was very dark, and I went on board unobserved, two hours before the time of departure. Going down into the saloon cabin, I saw the purser sitting near the entrance, to whom I said: "Parlez vous Français?" He shook his head. I then asked in jargon for "une billet a Glasgow." Surmising what I wished, he gave me a ticket, putting on it the number of my berth.

Expecting to be followed, I had taken that instant precaution of impressing on the purser's mind that I was a Frenchman. I passed into the wash-room, just opposite where the purser sat, washed myself, and brushed my hair. Just at this moment I heard steps descending the cabin stairway, then the words:

"Purser, a cab just brought a man from the Dublin train. Where is he?" "Oh, you mean the Frenchman," replied the purser; "he's in the wash-room."

While this was passing I had put on my silk hat and taken up my valise, and was standing before the glass (*à la Français*), taking a final view of my *toilette*, and snapping off some imaginary dust and lint, as two detectives stepped in, and after looking me well over, went out, and I saw them no more. That proved to be the last ordeal through which I passed in the hunt through Ireland. After being convinced that they had left the steamer, I went to my berth, and being thoroughly exhausted, I fell asleep in an instant, not awaking until the steamer was entering the harbor of Glasgow.

After my arrest a month later in Scotland, during the transfer to London, and afterward at Newgate, while awaiting trial four months, the detectives told me that they were in Cork three hours after I had left, and one of them related their adventures substantially as follows:

We arrived in Cork Saturday afternoon, and were not long in finding the temperance hotel where you stayed on Friday night, and the hat you left behind. After a long hunt we ascertained that a jaunting-car had left the stand some hours previously, and was still absent.

We had a good laugh at those blunder-heads, the Cork officers, letting you slip through their fingers, and then showed them how we do things. After some delay, we traced the cab across the bridge to the shop where you got the boy to go for it. The shopwoman was quite voluble about you, saying she knew all the time that you were an American by the accent, and described the bag and ulster which we had ascertained were in your possession. Of course we were now satisfied that we were on the right scent, but could get no further trace, or the direction taken by the cab. We therefore sent dispatches to all the telegraph stations within fifty miles to put the police on the watch, and sent messengers to the outlying places; but somehow you slipped through our meshes, and nothing turned up until the carman returned at about eleven P. M., as drunk as a soldier on furlough. After putting him under a water-tap until he was half drowned, we got him sober enough to tell where he had left you; but he swore you were a priest, and his evident sincerity caused us all to roar with laughter. This angered him, and he said: "Ye may twist me head an dhroun me intirely, but I wull niver spake another wurrud about the jintelman at all, at all," and sure enough, we could get nothing more out of him.

We had a carriage ready, and, jumping in, we were at the wayside inn by midnight, and terrified the old woman half out of her wits in arousing her out of bed. After a while she gathered them sufficiently to show us that you had six hours the start of us. The boy who carried your bag could give us no points, but we concluded you intended taking the branch line at Fermoy for Dublin. We drove right on, arriving at the Fermoy station at one A. M.; but getting no trace, we telegraphed to all the stations along the line to Dublin, and there as well, to be on the lookout. Who would ever have thought of your taking the opposite direction, penning yourself in at the end of a branch line, at a small, inland town like Lismore? Why, you were, as we discovered the next morning, at that moment sleeping quietly at the Lismore Hotel, and only about ten miles from where we were working so industriously for that £500! Well, you "done" us fine, that time!

After you so cleverly threw us off the trail, we could get no trace until Sunday morning, when we received a dispatch from Lismore, stating that a man had come on the last train, stayed at the hotel, and left at daylight without paying his bill; also, that he had left a bag in his room, which contained some collars marked "G. B." "Hello!" said I, as soon as I read the dispatch, "we never suspected Lismore; he has been there all night, and is off, again!" We telegraphed to Clonmel, Waterford, and other places; then left for Lismore, where we arrived, paid your bill, and took the bag with us. Surmising that you might make for Clonmel, we looked for and found the place where you got the car, but no news as to what direction you had taken. It would have made you laugh, as it did us, to see the old livery-man stamp about and tear his hair when he found how easily he could have made the £500 — if he had "only known."

Starting on the way to Clonmel, we soon had news which satisfied us we were once more on the right track. Shortly after we met, sure enough, the cab you had sent back from the country store. Arriving there we took the boy, who had just returned from driving you to Clonmel, with us, and feeling sure that we should soon come up with you, we made our horses spin toward that town. Arriving there, we saw the Inspector, who informed us that he had sent a constable in pursuit of a man who had hired a car to go to

Cahir. [This must have been one of the men in the car whom I escaped by dodging into the ruined cottage.—AUTHOR.] It being then sundown, we drove to Cahir, with all speed, arriving there just after dark, passing the Clonmel mail-car inside the gate ; but it contained no one but the driver. [It appears that the Bow detectives arrived just as I was going with Maloy through the lane, as previously described]

We soon found the constable sent from Clonmel, who said you had disappeared into the fort, where a friend must have concealed you, and that you must be there still. He then took us to the fort, which was closed for the night. As soon as my eyes lighted on the ruined cottages, I asked him if he had searched them, and received an answer in the negative. " Why," said he, "they are, as you see, all open to the day, without roof, doors, or windows, and no one would think of hiding in them." " You are a fool," I replied ; "Give me your lamp, and come in with me." After a look around, and seeing how easily any person could stand in a corner out of sight, I remarked to him, emphatically, that he was the biggest specimen of a goose I had ever seen in my line. " I think," said I, "you had better go home and play pin. Here is where he dodged you, and now he is off again, with an hour or more start !" We worked until after midnight, and gave Cahir such a " turning over " that the inhabitants won't soon forget, but could not get hold of the least trace, except at one place [Maloy's], where a woman said a stranger came in at supper-time, who said he was an American seeing the people in their homes. We cross-questioned the man, but could get nothing out of him more than that you had departed.

At last we gave it up, went to the hotel to get some sleep, which we needed badly, and the next day went to Dublin, heard about the finding of your neckwrapper at the Cathedral Hotel, and knocked about Ireland for some time. During this time we arrested several persons, but soon discovered none of them were the right party, and we never obtained a genuine trace until you gave yourself away later in Edinburgh.

Readers who may discover any trace of exultation in my relation of the cool and skillful manner in which I eluded the detectives, will bear in mind that the story is told from the standpoint of my then state of feeling. It is only fair for me to say that, at the moment, while in the thick of it, I did feel a certain exultation and full confidence in my ability to keep out of the way for all time. But my name had become known, which, with other disclosures, showed that I had been a victim of misplaced confidence ; and, though I might have gone anywhere with impunity, while they were still hunting me in Ireland, I lay dormant in Edinburgh rather than to be *hunted through the world.*

CHAPTER XII.

ARRIVAL IN EDINBURGH—A MYSTERY UNVEILED—EDITORIAL FROM THE "LONDON TIMES"—I AM ARRESTED—M'KELVIE AND McNAB—DIAMONDS—BAILIE WILSON—CROWDS TO SEE ME OFF—TRANSFERRED TO LONDON—A NIGHT AT BOW-STREET POLICE STATION—BEFORE THE LORD MAYOR OF LONDON—THE MANSION HOUSE—CONSIGNED TO NEWGATE.

ON arrival of the steamer at Glasgow, about three A. M., it was a question whether I ought not to go directly back to London, and, while it was believed I was still in Ireland, make a rush across the Channel, through France to Marseilles, then by steamer to Rio Janeiro. On arrival there it would be easy to take one of the coast line steamships for New York. But, feeling that my escape from Ireland had cut off all trace of me, I concluded to take the train to Edinburgh and lie by for a while. Arriving there I stayed one night at a small temperance hotel, assuming the character of a German, and the next day I took a room at 22 Cumberland Street—a lodging house for medical students. Here I remained from the 10th of March until the 3d of April, sometimes passing the day in wandering about this interesting ancient city. A stroll through the old Edinburgh streets, and the old Market Cross, furnished material for reflection on the vicissitudes of life as illustrated in the pictures of the past, which filled my mind as I gazed upon these relics of generations in whose footsteps I was now treading.

It had all along been a great mystery to me as to how the detectives had so easily unveiled the actors, and so quickly ascertained the connection of McDonald and myself with the forgery. But now having access to the newspapers, shock after shock nearly overwhelmed me as I saw how I had been duped to take part in a crime without the slightest chance of keeping it enveloped in the darkness in which I firmly believed it was wrapped. But enough on that point. The object of this book is not to inculpate—still less to exonerate myself

OLD EDINBURGH STREET.

from the justifiable charge of having been a fool.

On arriving in London, I was taken to the Bow-street Police Station and put into a cell, to pass a sleepless night, and about ten the next morning, made my first appearance in the Mansion House before Mayor Sir Sidney Waterlow. After some preliminary sparring between the lawyers, I was consigned to Newgate, to ruminate upon my gradual descent into that hades. — two days after my arrest in Edinboro.

BOW STREET POLICE STATION.

Chapter XIII.

EXTRADITION OF AUSTIN FROM CUBA AND GEORGE McDONALD FROM NEW YORK—AUSTIN ARRESTED IN HAVANA—A "NEW YORK HERALD" EDITORIAL—SYMPATHY WITH "FILLIBUSTERS"—CABLE DISPATCHES TO "THE HERALD" AND "THE LONDON TIMES"—GENERAL SICKLES'S INTERVIEW WITH SENOR CASTELAR AT MADRID—BIDWELL ESCAPES—RECAPTURE—HE IS SURRENDERED TO THE BRITISH GOVERNMENT—ARRIVAL IN ENGLAND—McDONALD ARRIVES IN NEW YORK—DETECTIVES IRVING AND FARLEY TRICK SHERIFF JUDSON JARVIS—BOARD THE "THURINGIA" AT QUARANTINE—CURIOUS "SEARCH" OF McDONALD—SHERIFFS JARVIS AND CURRY TOO LATE—NO BONDS RECOVERED—SEIZE WATCHES AND DIAMONDS—McDONALD AT LUDLOW STREET JAIL—EXTRADITION PROCEEDINGS—STARTLING ARREST OF SUPERINTENDENT KELSO AND DETECTIVES IRVING AND FARLEY—McDONALD'S RIDE DOWN BROADWAY—IN FORT COLUMBUS—SURRENDERED TO THE BRITISH GOVERNMENT—EXIT ON STEAMSHIP "MINNESOTA"—THE "DOMINION'S SELFISH PROTECTION OF BANK DEFAULTERS, BOODLERS," ETC.

IT will be remembered that in Chapter was detailed the imprudent marriage of my brother, and his arrest at Havana while on his wedding journey.

I now resume the story, giving in this chapter some account, from contemporary sources, of his extradition from Cuba and his arrival in London.

[Editorial *N. Y. Herald*, March 29, 1873.]

CUBAN AFFAIRS—BIDWELL'S IMPRISONMENT.

The special telegraph advices which we publish to-day in reference to the imprisonment at Havana of Bidwell, one of the parties accused of the recent forgeries on the Bank of England, are very interesting, touching the jurisdiction of the Island authorities in this matter. It appears that Bidwell was arrested at the request of the British government, on the supposition that he was a British subject; but it is represented that he is a citizen of the United States of America, a native of Michigan, and that his arrest in Cuba is not justified by any extradition treaty with England nor by any other authority, except that of the Captain-General, whose will over the Island is the supreme law. If it can be established that Bidwell is a citizen of the United States, his case certainly calls for the intervention of Mr. Secretary Fish. The prisoner, it seems, desires a transfer to New York, which is perfectly natural; *but we suspect that the international difficulties* suggested, touching his detention in Cuba, will not materially improve his chances of escape.

Not long before the arrest of my brother in Cuba, the steamer *Virginia*, an American vessel, was captured by a Spanish cruiser. On the charge of being "fillibusters," the crew and all persons found on board were shot. Among these were several Americans. The United States government sent for the *Virginia* and demanded reparation for her capture, and indemnity for the lives of the Americans. This was the cause of serious international complications, which threatened to end in war. It was this state of affairs referred to in the italics of the *Herald* editorial above quoted, which caused his final surrender.

There is no longer any doubt that the punctilious Spaniards would never have surrendered Austin   to the demand of the British government, had it not been for their posture of hostility toward the United States. There was considerable ground for this feeling in the sympathy shown in some parts of the United States for, and assistance rendered to, the Cuban insurgents.

It will be perceived, by the following dispatch, that Austin was supposed to be a British subject.

[Telegrams to the *New York Herald* of 29th, referred to in above editorial.]

HAVANA, March 26, 1873.

The man Bidwell was, it appears, arrested on the charge of complicity with the forgeries on the Bank of England, at the request of the British government, communicated to the Captain-General of Cuba by the Spanish Ministers in London and Washington, who supposed him to be a British subject. Bidwell is, on the contrary, an American, a native of Michigan. His arrest is not justified by any treaty of extradition between Spain, England, or the United States. Such proceedings could be carried out in no other country than Cuba, where the Captain-General does not always act in accordance with law. Distinguished lawyers and judges of this city, in conversation with the *Herald* correspondent, denounce the act as being utterly illegal, and without precedent, except in the case of Argeumes, in the year 1864.

COMMON LAW AND TREATY SET AT DEFIANCE.

The gentlemen also declare that it is a violation of the laws of Spain and of the treaty stipulations with the United States, and in contempt of the guarantees of the law of 1870 relative to foreigners. The same lawyers and judges assert that it would be better that a delinquent should escape than that so bad a precedent as the act of delivery of Bidwell would make should be established.

THE PRISONER'S TREATMENT AND FEARS.

Bidwell has been now seven days incommunicated — not permitted to see a lawyer or his wife. The *Herald* correspondent has been refused permission to see him.

The British Vice-Consul obtained, by compulsion, the sum of $5,000 from Mrs. Bidwell, in United States five-twenties. Complaints having been made, the Captain-General ordered that the sum should be deposited.

Bidwell is afraid that there exist no guarantees for a due and proper administration of justice here. He has expressed his desire to be sent to New York.

[Cable dispatches from Havana to the *London Times*.]

NEW YORK, April 4, 1873.

Great efforts are being made by the lawyers to obtain the release of Bidwell, and an action for illegal arrest is threatened.

HAVANA, April 4th.

The American Consul here demands from the Cuban authorities the release of the prisoner Bidwell, *alias* Warren, on the ground that he is an American citizen.

MADRID, April 8th.

Gen. Sickles has formally notified Senor Castelar that the American government will consent to the surrender to the British government of Bidwell, now in custody in Havana, upon a charge of being concerned in the forgeries upon the Bank of England.

HAVANA, April 10th.

The British Consul continues to counteract the efforts that are being made to prevent the extradition of Bidwell.

Generals Portello and Renegassi have been relieved of their posts, and are ordered to return to Spain. (For opposing Austin extradition).

[By cable from Havana to *N. Y. Herald*, April 13, 1873.]

Bidwell, the alleged Bank of England forger, escaped yesterday by jumping over the balcony. He was partly dressed. He is supposed to be hiding in this city. Bidwell's Havana friends, seeing the impossibility of counteracting by legal means the efforts of the British Consul to secure his extradition, undoubtedly planned the affair.

HAVANA, April 14th.

Bidwell has been recaptured on the seashore twenty miles above Havana. He was severely bruised in the hands and legs while escaping from prison. He had leaped from under the soldiers' bayonets, from the Arsenal second story into the crowded street, and got clear out of Havana without assistance.

[By cable to the *London Times*.]

HAVANA, April 17, 1873.

While Inspectors Hayden and Green, and a clerk of the Bank of England, were on their passage from New York to Havana, a notorious thief, named Wilson, opened the detectives' trunks and extracted some money. His object is said to have been to secure the documents relating to the extradition of Bidwell. Wilson has been arrested on a charge of burglary. The English detectives and the British Consul have completely baffled the efforts to obtain the release of Bidwell.

[From the *London Times*, May 28, 1873.]

Among the passengers who landed at Plymouth yesterday afternoon, from the Royal Mail Company's steamship *Moselle*, were Austin   alias Warren, in charge of detectives Sergeants Michael Hayden and William Green, of the city police, and Mr. Curton, private detective (of Mr. Pinkerton's staff, from Chicago). They were joined at Plymouth by detective Sergeant John Moss of the city police, who had come down from London the previous night to meet the steamer. It being known at Plymouth that Bidwell was expected from Havana in the *Moselle*, a large number of persons assembled on Milbay pier, to await the return of the steam-tender with the mail, in order to get a sight of the prisoner, and so great was the crowd that it was with some difficulty that Bidwell and his escort managed to reach a cab and were driven to the Duke of Cornwall Hotel, adjoining the railway station. They left by the 7.45 P. M. mail train for London. A large crowd was present to see them off. Mr. Good, from the western branch of the Bank of England, who went to Jamaica to identify the prisoner, also came home in the *Moselle*, and went on in the steamer to Southampton, *en route* for London. Bidwell will be taken before the Lord Mayor at the Justice-room of the Mansion House this morning.

I have it from what I consider the best authority, that among the secret stipulations of the treaty for settling the steamer *Virginia* affair — in which Great Britain had a hand — was one in effect binding the United States government to consent that Austin might be delivered to the British authorities by the Spanish government.

I would call the especial attention of our neighbors of the "Dominion" to the foregoing. On this occasion it was an American — to whom the laws of his own country properly refused protection, after the committal of a crime abroad — who was extradited from Cuba, despite the fact that there was no extradition treaty between Spain and England. It makes a difference whose bull is gored.

Long previous to 1873, a British dependency (or independency?) has been a safe refuge for bank-defaulters, boodlers, etc., from the United States — and this because of the dishonest money they squander or invest in the "Dominion." Short-sighted policy! Will not reflection convince our neighbors that seeing criminal "exiles" strutting about their towns in stolen plumes, living in high style, and squandering their illicit gains in divers ways, is a direct incentive to their young men to "go and do likewise"? Such a blind policy is sure to entail its own retribution, with compound interest, and even now we have a Canadian colony of the same kidney protected by the starry flag.

In Chapter   I gave a sketch of McDonald's flight and embarkation at Havre for New York. As soon as the *Thuringia* was fairly on her voyage he felt comparatively safe, believing that even if the fact transpired that he was one of my party, it would be impossible to extradite him from New York.

But before the steamer arrived Mr. Kelso, then superintendent of the New York City police, received a cablegram from Inspector Bailey of the City of London police, with full particulars, and at once detailed Detectives Irving and Farley to meet the steamer and arrest McDonald.

At the same time the law firm of Blatchford, Seward & Da Costa, agents for the Bank of England, received the same information, also that McDonald had a large sum in bonds and other valuables. They at once procured a writ of attachment from the Supreme Court which they confided to Sheriff Brennan for execution.

Commissioner Gutman appointed Detective Irving United States Deputy Marshal to serve the warrant against McDonald. The action of the plaintiff's attorneys made the police officers responsible for the person of McDonald on the criminal charge, and held Sheriff Brennan responsible for the seizure and attachment of all the valuables and property found upon him. It became important, therefore, that the police and sheriff's officers should act jointly, and arrangements were made for both police detectives and sheriff's deputies to go together down the bay to meet the incoming steamer. Therefore, Detectives Farley and Irving, Deputy Sheriff Judson Jarvis, and special Deputy Lawrence Curry, went down the bay on Tuesday, March 18th, on board the police boat *Seneca*, and prepared to board her from the quarantine boat. The detectives and Deputy Sheriff Jarvis had gone ashore for this purpose, leaving special Deputy Curry on board the police boat, which was in charge of a sergeant.

The detectives before going aboard the quarantine boat urged Deputy Sheriff Judson Jarvis to remain on shore until they sent for him, alleging that they feared the forger might divine the object of their visit, and make away with the bonds which it was certain he had on his person. Their real object was to see him alone first, as they knew he would confide *his valuables to them for safe-keeping*. Ponder on the import of those italics. This the deputy declined to do, and went aboard the quarantine boat with them, but on attempting to board the *Thuringia* at the same time with the detectives, Mr. Jarvis was prevented by Dr. Moshier, deputy Health Officer in charge, although insisting on his right as a sheriff serving an order of the Supreme Court. The detectives with whom the deputy sheriff was acting in concert, of course, made no attempt to explain to the Health Officer, but hurrying below got from Mac, with whom they were well-acquainted, all the bonds in his possession, while Deputy Sheriff Jarvis was thus prevented from executing the order of the Supreme Court.

Meantime special Deputy Curry, on board the police boat, becoming suspicious from the long delay that something was wrong on board the *Thuringia*, requested the sergeant to run down alongside the steamer, and a rope being thrown him, he immediately climbed on board. Finding that his superior had been detained on the health boat, he immediately ran to the other side, and assuming authority, ordered the boat forward, and Deputy Sheriff Jarvis sprang up the side of the vessel, and both officers at once went below. The *search* of McDonald, of course, had been concluded, when the sheriff's entered the state-room and made the attachment of what little property was found. This consisted of about $10,000 in gold, that being too heavy for the detectives to carry away, and it would have been dangerous to attempt to make way with the watches and diamonds, Mac having displayed them on the voyage,— two gold watches, one diamond ring weighing ten karats and worth probably $10,000, two diamonds weighing four and one-sixteenth karats, and one diamond weighing four and one-half karats. Not a single bond of any description was found by the sheriff, and only a few gold coins were left on Mac's person. On being searched a second time McDonald laughed and said, "I'm clean; you can't prove anything on me; you can't send me back to England on any such charge."

In order to throw dust in the eyes of the sheriff, the detectives pretended to become suspicious of others on board, and at their suggestion, the custom-house officers searched the person of one named Philip D'Artigue who had come aboard at Havre, and who had been frequently in conversation with Mac during the voyage. It was rumored on board that he had 300,000 francs on his person when he started, but no bonds of any description or money were found on him. Other passengers were searched but none of the bonds were found, and McDonald was taken to the Ludlow Street house-of-detention.

After depositing the captured property in safe keeping, Deputy Sheriff Jarvis reported the seizure that had been made to Messrs. Blatchford, Seward & Da Costa. Those lawyers were astonished at the result of the search, which disappointed their well-grounded expectations. Inquiry was made by them into the circumstances of the deputy sheriff's detention, and they asked his opinion of the proceedings, but this he declined to give.

Finally, after consultation among themselves, they directed the deputy sheriff to serve the same warrant of attachment he had served upon Mac, upon Detectives Irving and Farley; also on Superintendent Kelso. After some hesitation and inquiry of his own counsel, the deputy sheriff found it was incumbent upon him to take this extraordinary and unusual proceeding. He therefore repaired, about six o'clock P. M., to the office of the superintendent, and immediately served an attachment on him and on Detectives Farley and Irving. The service of the writ on Superintendent Kelso was a great surprise to him. This service rendered all three subject to examination about the bonds.

During the extradition proceedings before United States Commissioner Gutman, Superintendent Kelso purged himself and his subordinates, Detectives Farley and Irving (who skillfully evaded examination on the ground that their superior, Superintendent Kelso, was responsible for their acts and must answer for them, they reporting detective services only to him), from the implied charge of having appropriated bonds, etc., by making oath that he had nothing "except a revolver taken from the possession of the said George McDonald."

I am not able to say that the superintendent was in the confidence of his subordinates, in the case in question; but I do know, on the best authority, that the two detectives did take a considerable amount of United States bonds from Mac on board the steamer, and that the whole object of their maneuvering to prevent the deputy sheriffs, Judson Jarvis and Lawrence Curry, from getting on board the steamer at the same time with themselves, was for the express purpose of affording them that opportunity. I could give some startling particulars in regard to this and cognate matters — but let it pass.

Mr. E. M. Archibald, British Consul, made a demand on the part of his government for the surrender of McDonald, and had orders to aid the Bank of England agents, Messrs. Blatchford, Seward & Da Costa, in procuring his extradition. Mr. J. R. Fellows, the present District Attorney of New York City, Charles W. Brooke, and Mr. J. R. Dos Passos acted as counsel for McDonald.

The legal proceedings lasted from the 20th of March to the 5th of June, 1873. The array of counsel on both sides made it a forensic contest between giants, in which all past history was invoked for precedents, pro and con. These two extradition cases caused international complications, in which ambassadors and consuls took an active part. I have the McDonald case complete in all its details, but not the space to record the full legal proceedings.

After United States Commissioner Gutman had finally

decided to surrender him to the demand of the British government, appeal was made to the United States Circuit Court, Judge Woodruff, then to the Supreme Court, Judge Barrett, before whom McDonald was brought by writs of *habeas corpus;* but the commissioner's decision was sustained, McDonald was sent to Fort Columbus for safe keeping, while counsel were vainly arguing on new writs of *habeas corpus* and *certiorari*, and before any conclusion could be reached, he was hurried away by his custodians. He had scarcely time to bid good-bye to his counsel, when he was handcuffed to a United States officer, and with him crowded into a carriage in Chambers Street, guarded by Chief Deputy Marshal Kennedy and Deputies Robinson and Crowley, and driven rapidly down Broadway to the Battery, so that the large crowd who gathered to witness his departure from the metropolis had very little time to feast their eyes.

McDonald was lively and chatty during the ride, smoked his Havana, and looked through the windows of the barouche as freely as if his hands were unshackled. He was transferred from the battery to Governor's Island by a tugboat, and subsequently handed over by the deputy marshals to the charge of Major J. P. Roy, who had him escorted to Fort Columbus, and saw him placed in one of the casemates, under the vigilance and charge of two guardsman and the surveillance of Deputy Marshal Robinson, and the English detective, Mr. Webb. Lieutenant J. W. Bean had him furnished with necessary requirements, and the deputy marshal and English detective with sleeping apartments near by.

The following morning, United States Marshal Fiske, with Deputies Crowley and Purvis, Mr. Peter Williams, solicitor of the Bank of England, Sergeant Edward Hancock, a London detective, Deputy Marshal Colfax, and others, boarded the steam-tug *P. C. Schultze* at the Battery, and steamed across to Governor's Island. At half-past ten o'clock, Captain J. W. Bean, on post at the fort, received through Major J. P. Roy the following order from United States Marshal Fiske:

MAJOR J. P. ROY, *United States Army, Commanding Fort Columbus:*
SIR, — You will please deliver to Deputy United States Marshal John Robinson, the prisoner George McDonald, now in custody, and oblige, OLIVER FISKE, *United States Marshal.*

On receipt of the above official notice Captain Bean prepared to deliver up the prisoner to the charge of United States Marshal Fiske and his party, who had by this time arrived at Fort Columbus, and were waiting at the doors of the casemate. The sentries paced the iron balconies with uninterrupted attention to duty, apparently unconcerned about the exigency on hand.

McDonald immediately recognized his visitors and understood the object of their visit, greeting them cordially as they entered the gloomy corridor. He looked, as usual, in good spirits, with some slight furrows of trouble and care upon his forehead, and a sort of distressing and affected mood of indifference in his deportment.

Captain J. W. Bean read to him the order of United States Marshal Fiske to Major J. P. Roy, and then delivered him over to United States Marshal Fiske's charge, with whom he descended the steps from the balcony of the fort, and marched, with a deputy at either side, through the tiled pathways and groved and shaded avenues, to the wharf at the other end of the island, where the *Schultze* was awaiting his arrival. A large crowd of spectators, soldiers, and civilians lined the wharf, lingering anxiously to see McDonald " off." But Mac walked very leisurely, smoked, laughed, and appeared in a state of unaccountable good humor. He reached the *Schultze* barge, however, in due time, shook hands with the deputies, marshals, sergeants, and detectives, and then went on board, and entered into conversation of some trivial kind with Messrs. Williams, Hancock, and Webb.

It was nearly eleven o'clock when the *Schultze* steamed away from Governor's Island wharf and whistled and rattled down the bay to await the arrival of the *Minnesota*, which lay at anchor during the forenoon near pier 46, North River, and did not sail until some minutes after twelve o'clock. The *Schultze* meantime waited, steaming around the lower bay until the *Minnesota* arrived. It was after half-past one o'clock. The sun was burning hot, and the browned and florid complexion of all showed its effects. The steam-tug neared the bulky and huge vessel, and McDonald was finally taken on board by United States Marshal Fiske and Deputy Marshals Robinson, Crowley, and Colfax, and given into the custody of the English detectives, Sergeants Webb and Hancock, who in return gave the usual receipt to Marshal Fiske.

For the present, I leave Mac on the Atlantic, sailing swiftly eastward, to meet his terrible doom.

A fitting finale to these remarkable extradition cases will be the following adventure, in which one of the English detectives figured rather ingloriously.

The three Bow-Street officers, Inspectors Hayden, Hancock, and Webb, expressed a desire to detectives Irving and Farley to be shown the sights of New York. Accordingly, these, acting in an unofficial capacity, accompanied their English visitors upon a night's round of the most notorious resorts. Previous to starting, however, the English officers were advised to leave their watches and other valuables at the hotel, lest they should be stolen during the excursion. But Hayden, who was to sail for Havana a few days later to arrest Bidwell, scorned the idea, and set out for his night's amusement.

Towards morning he became sleepy, and taking a nap, he subsequently discovered that he had been robbed, not only of his watch and pocketbook, but also of the papers for the extradition of Bidwell, which he had foolishly carried in his pocket. Of course, he was greatly dismayed at the loss of these important documents, but they were returned to him by Superintendent Kelso, who had received them from Capt. Leary of the City Hall precinct. They had been surreptitiously left at the station-house on the day following the robbery. The watch and pocketbook were not recovered.

CHAPTER XIV.

FIRST NIGHT IN NEWGATE — GOVERNOR JONAS — EXERCISE AT NEWGATE — DR. KENEALY — MR. GEORGE LEWIS — DAVID HOWELL, A "PATTERN" SOLICITOR — A FATAL CONCESSION ON MY PART — DON'T "SWOP HORSES WHILE CROSSING A STREAM" — HOWELL "FEES" BARRISTERS FOR US — HIS "MANAGEMENT" OF OUR CASE — HOWELL "HOLDS" MY DIAMOND STUDS — 108 WITNESSES — VISITORS AT NEWGATE — HOWELL'S "BENEVOLENT" CALLS — MISTAKEN IDENTIFICATION — LONDON ALDERMEN — ANOTHER PHASE OF "LIFE IN NEWGATE," FROM "THE LONDON TIMES" — CAGED ANIMALS — ALFRED DE ROTHSCHILD AND ONE OF HIS "FAMILIARS" — VISIT FROM THE RUSSIAN PRINCE IMPERIAL, THE PRESENT CZAR — LORD MAYOR WATERLOW AGAIN — THE PRINCE'S RETINUE — I CONTEMPLATE RETURNING HIS CALL AT ST. PETERSBURGH.

TO be sure, I was not to be hanged, as was the man at that moment sitting on the bench in the "condemned cell" in the same ward. But that first night in Newgate! A sleepless one, indeed — given up to retrospections and vain regrets. I at last had reached that dread abode of which I had read so much; that place, the scene of so many horrors in the dim and misty past, whose history, extending over a period of eight hundred years — one long record of crime — had rendered the very name infamous. While lying restless on the pallet, with closed eyes, my mind wandered in a chaos until I almost fancied myself the victim of an oppressive nightmare. Opening them upon the cheerless surroundings, as seen by the gas-light shining dimly through the glass plate imbedded in the wall, dissipated the illusion, and the whole horror of my position surged anew through my seething brain. Toward morning, dropping off into fitful slumbers, I dreamed of happier days, only to awake each time with a start, to realize more fully the degradation I had brought upon myself.

The next morning the governor (warden he would be called in the States) of Newgate, Mr. Jonas, since dead, came into my cell and said that if I did not wish to live on the jail fare, I could have food brought in from a restaurant, to the amount of half a crown per day — sixty cents' worth — at

CONDEMNED TO BE HANGED.

my own cost. I thought this rather a small allowance, but Mr. Jonas explained that the jail regulations permitted no more.

Governor Jonas also informed me that in anticipation of my arrival he had put a cot bed in the cell for me to sleep on, instead of the sailor's hammock, which hangs from the side walls, and which, afterwards, I found so difficult a contrivance to sleep in, and so easy to fall out of. Soon after I was taken to the doctor, who asked me if there was anything he could do for me; but I declined his services, with thanks. In the afternoon I was taken into the inner court, (see illustration, page 33), for an hour's exercise, and a motley crew they were, walking round and round the court. While there, detectives came in every day to see if they could detect

NEWGATE.—PREPARING FOR AN EXECUTION.

among the "new chums" any old offenders, and seldom failed to call out several, as shown in the following cut.

Not knowing any solicitor in London, I sent for George Lewis, whose name I had seen in the newspapers in connection with criminal trials. The next day Noyes and myself were again before the Lord Mayor at the Mansion House, and after some sparring between Dr. Kenealy and Mr. G. Lewis on our behalf, and Mr. Freshfield on the part of the Bank, we were once more remanded to our cells in Newgate.

A DETECTIVE IDENTIFYING OLD OFFENDERS AT NEWGATE.

As some of my readers may not understand the distinction between solicitors and barristers, it may be well to explain that the solicitor takes the case and transacts all the business connected with it. A barrister is the lawyer who is employed by the solicitor to argue and conduct the case in court. He does not come in direct contact with the prisoner, but gets his instructions from the solicitor — all this being different from the system pursued in our own country.

When Noyes found himself so unexpectedly in the grasp of the British Lion, not knowing any other solicitor, he sent for Howell, the man who had charged him so exorbitant a fee for the articles of agreement between himself and "Horton." It was precisely this that prevented me from sending for him, on the principle that "a straw shows which way the wind blows," and it would have been well if on this and other occasions I had "stuck to my text."

Although, very properly, talking was by the Newgate rules prohibited, still, like many other prison "prohibitions," this was evaded. Noyes being with me in the same courtyard at exercise, asked me to give up Mr. Lewis and employ Howell, so that we could communicate safely with each other through him. To this I demurred, because my one interview with the former gentleman, together with his admirable conduct upon the occasion of our first examination at the Mansion House, had convinced me that he was not only a skillful but also a straightforward lawyer. However, Noyes arranged with Howell to have me called into the consulting-room. On entering, I saw before me an under-sized, spare man, with a sandy complexion, red hair, small, covetous eyes, and the general air of a Shylock; and when he spoke, it was in a squeaky voice. After some preliminaries, he began to insinuate various things against Mr. Lewis, speaking of him as that "sheeney" (Jew), etc. Of course the strain of the previous days had somewhat affected my judgment, and to oblige Noyes I finally agreed to transfer my case into his hands. And a fatal concession it was.

I have often wondered since, what possessed me to "swop horses while crossing the stream," especially as I had that famous saying of "Honest old Abe" in mind at the moment. Mr. Lewis would have guarded against the occurrences which caused us to get the life sentences.

At this juncture another brother, John an honest man, arrived in England, and brought with him some bonds — United States seven-thirties — to use in our defense. Not being posted in money matters, he placed $4,000 in Howell's hands for him to sell, and use the proceeds in engaging barristers of the highest standing for our defense.

EXAMINATION OF BIDWELL AND NOYES BEFORE THE LORD MAYOR OF LONDON.

On one of Howell's daily visits to Newgate to see us, he sounded me as to the price I thought he ought to receive for the bonds. Upon my asking him what he could sell them for, he said he had credited them at a price which was thirty per cent. under the market rate. I soon undeceived him as to his idea of our ignorance on that point, by informing him of the fact that John had sold, by my direction, since the $4,000 was put into his hands, another lot of bonds for the full market price. This incident is only an introduction to others regarding this "pattern" solicitor, the reading of which will, I think, please and amuse Mr. Freshfield, the Bank of England solicitor, and the barristers whom Mr. Howell engaged to defend us.

After he had received the $4,000, and £300 Mr. Lewis had paid into his hands, he applied in open court for an allowance for our defense, to be paid out of funds taken away from us, on the ground that he had received nothing from us, and consequently could not pay the barristers. Accordingly the judge ordered that £100 for each one of us four should be refunded. We had directed Solicitor Howell to secure the services of barristers who stood high in their profession, such as Mr. Powell, Q. C. (Queen's Counsel), Mr. Besley, Mr. McIntire, Q. C., Mr. Moody, Mr. Ribton, and Mr. Hollings; and to pay the Q. Cs. each £100 or £150 fees, and the others in proportion. During the trial I ascertained that Howell had, instead of payment, enlisted their sympathies, and on the ground that he had only the £300 allowed by the court to the three of us whom he represented — McDonald having wisely secured the services of an honorable solicitor, St. John Wentner — induced them to work almost for nothing.

We being foreigners, and the case an important one, the barristers stepped over the usual bounds and took suggestions directly from us, an example of which may be seen in the illustration, page   in which McDonald is speaking with his barrister, Mr. Straight. They are very good likenesses of the lawyer and client in 1873.

Before being arrested, I had sent Mr. George Lewis £300, to use in the defense of Noyes. To show the difference between Mr. Lewis and Howell — who spoke disparagingly of him and took the meanest course to get my case out of his hands, as previously mentioned — when Mr. Lewis ascertained that Noyes had already sent for Howell, he paid over to the latter the £300, instead of showing my note to Noyes, which would have secured the case and the £300 to himself. It will be seen by the above that at the time Solicitor Howell applied for an allowance of money, he had above £1,000 in his hands, which, with the £300 allowed by the court, made £1,300, the greater part of which he applied to his own use and benefit, paying out but a small part of it in the preparation of a proper defense. He managed the case on our side, according to my observations, exactly as Mr. Freshfield would have desired in order to carry out the latter's theory, exonerating the Bank managers from a charge of neglect, etc., as elsewhere explained.

A copy of the book of depositions taken before the Lord Mayor was given to me by Solicitor Howell, with the request that I would memorandum on the broad margin left for the purpose, any criticisms of the evidence I might wish to make for the guidance of the lawyers. Accordingly I worked at it from the close of the examination, the 2d of July, during a month, and showed where the witnesses against me had contradicted themselves — engravers swearing they had engraved letters which appeared on the false bills, that I could have proved another had actually done, etc. — so that their evidence must have been thrown out. Yet Solicitor Howell suppressed all this. I also gave him an order for a set of diamond studs, valued at $1,000, to hold for me, and he has "held" them ever since. A few moments previous to the sentence I ascertained that he had received them, and was then wearing them in his shirt-front. They were set in black enamel, and doubtless our barristers whom he defrauded out of their just fees may have since observed what a sparkling

ONE WHO HAS BEEN ROBBED IDENTIFYING THE THIEF AT NEWGATE.

light in the profession he had suddenly become. These and other circumstances convinced me, before the eight days trial at the Old Bailey was half over, that Solicitor Howell was playing into the hands of the prosecution, and, to prevent discovery of his malappropriation of money and valuables to the amount of $10,000, connived to get us put out of the way for life — especially me, whom he feared had penetrated his designs.

All this was so clear that on the seventh day of the trial I determined to get up in open court and expose the whole matter, but on taking counsel with one of the barristers he dissuaded me from my purpose. I hope that he used the information I then gave him to extract from Solicitor Howell just fees for himself and his brother barristers.

It was Solicitor Howell who gave Governor Jonas information, exaggerating something I said to him, thus causing the great scare during the trial about an alleged plan of escape.

During the five horrible months I was awaiting trial, it was a great relief to be called out of my cell into the consulting-room every day to pass five or ten minutes with Solicitor Howell, and for a long time my opinion of his character as first formed was modified by such a proof of his considerate kindness. But after he had made about one hundred visits I ascertained that he was charging ten dollars each visit, though I had on several occasions endeavored to ascertain whether he was charging for them, but was put off with a laugh and the remark: "O, I have business in the jail."

It was a relief to be called out of my cell, no matter for what purpose. Upon several occasions I was turned out into the yard with a dozen other prisoners, as shown in illustration, page 65, in order that a person or persons should be compelled to point out from among a number the one against whom he was to testify, or whom he accused of some offense. Of course the above way is a fair one to accused and accuser, and is the usual plan in England; but in my own case, on more than one occasion, some one of the one hundred and eight witnesses were brought to identify me while I stood in the dock at the Mansion House, many of whom professed to having seen us but once or twice several weeks or months previously.

Another great relief from the monotony of my cell was the advent of a visitor. In the illustration, page   are seen the prisoners with their faces pressed against the wire grating — the meshes being about one-quarter inch square — talking to their friends who have come to visit them, the space between the two wire gratings being four feet. An officer stands at one end or paces back and forth in this space to prevent any small article or written communication from being passed across by use of a slender cane or wire, etc. But I found that there, as elsewhere, a judicious application of "backsheesh" would enable me to pass to my relative such private instructions as I did not wish other eyes to see. I took pleasure in evading such an unjust restriction, preventing prisoners who had not even been examined, indicted, tried, or convicted — in many cases only held on suspicion — from communicating freely with their friends. Prisoners are not permitted to see the newspapers, and are kept wholly in the dark as to what is going on in the world, just the same as if they were already convicts.

In our own country all this is different. A prisoner confined in jail awaiting trial is permitted all proper indulgences, such as visits without listeners, food, fruit, newspapers, etc. Even in the Tombs, the New York city prison — that well-named sink of iniquity — visitors are admitted to stand at the cell door, as seen in the illustration, and talk to their heart's content. The bars leave spaces of four or five inches square so that the visitor can at least squeeze the fingers of the incarcerated friend. To show the difference: Being rather dyspeptic I felt the need of some fruit, and when Governor Jonas made his round one day I asked him to let some fruit be purchased for me, with some of my money then in his

PRISONERS WAITING TRIAL, AT NEWGATE, RECEIVING VISITORS.

possession. He informed me that it was not in his power to grant my request, and referred me to the visiting magistrate, I think Alderman Sir Robert Carden, saying that he would bring him to me when he came to the prison. A day or two later my cell door was thrown open and in stepped the governor accompanied by the alderman. I stated my want, and after some conversation, he wound up by saying: "I can see that you are a gentleman, and I will talk to the governor about it, but such a thing has not hitherto been permitted."

Whatever may have been the nature of his subsequent conversation with Mr. Jonas, I got no fruit, and I think I have remarked elsewhere that from the moment of my arrest to my discharge, nearly fifteen years later, the only "fruit" I ever had consisted of potatoes and cabbage. Think of that, ye gourmands, and beware!

The following extract from the *London Times* of July 2, 1873, illustrates another phase of life in Newgate:

(Extract from the last day's examination before the Lord Mayor.)

THE PRISONERS, GEORGE AND AUSTIN
EDWIN NOYES, AND GEORGE McDONALD,
AT THE MANSION HOUSE.

The prisoner George Bidwell said he had an application to make to his Lordship (Mayor Waterlow). He had now been three months in Newgate, undergoing the most rigorous solitary confinement, and on twenty-three occasions he had been pilloried in that dock. His position was greatly saddened by the fact that one who was so near and dear to him as his brother was should have been placed at his side on the same charge, and under circumstances which he desired to say were caused by himself alone. His brother was many years his junior, and owing to family misfortunes, he and several others had been placed, when quite young, under his charge (G. B's). He found, according to the rules of Newgate, two persons were sometimes permitted to occupy the same cell during some part of the day, and he asked that the privilege be granted to him and his brother. He appealed to his Lordship that this last boon — this last gleam of sunshine which they might ever be permitted to enjoy, — might be granted, — remembering that, in case of conviction, they would be forever separated from each other. It would be impossible for him to long survive the imprisonment which would follow a conviction. Austin also made the same request.

VISITOR TRYING ON THE HANGMAN'S IRON PINIONING BELT AT NEWGATE.

The Lord Mayor said it rested not with him, but with the visiting justices, who were this month Aldermen Sir William Rose and Lusk.

The prisoner Noyes applied that a small ring given him by his sister before he left America should be returned to him. He had not applied before because he expected to be free. The Lord Mayor ordered it to be returned to him."

In accordance with the Lord Mayor's statement I had applied to the alderman above named, but my application failed — they avoiding a direct refusal by an "I'll see about it," which I afterward found to be the hackneyed phrase regarding most applications. From July 2d, until August 18th, we were kept rigorously secluded, and though we were to be tried together, could have no opportunity for concerting a mutual defense. Had we been permitted to be together a few hours more or less every day, I could have prevented Austin from being taken in by the warders' imaginary plan of escape from Newgate. We were not even permitted to exercise in the same court-yard together.

I was "favored" — people are curious to see caged animals of all descriptions — with numerous calls, not of the exact kind depicted in the accompanying cut, where the gentleman is trying on the hangman's irons for the "amusement" of the ladies, but from some of the "great guns" of the universe; men, but for whose aid the world would cease to revolve, judging by the way some people cringe to their superiors in wealth — perhaps inferiors in all other qualifications.

One day, soon after my arrival in Newgate, a warder unlocked my cell door, and informed me that I was wanted in the consulting-room. Upon entering, I saw two men of the most opposite appearance — evidently a god and a demon. Alfred de Rothschild was a well-built man, above the medium height, with auburn hair, blue eyes, and a rather pleasing expression of countenance, save that he looked as though he had been up late nights. He had the air of a gentleman, and I found him possessed of the manners and language characteristic of one, whatever his worldly circumstances. He was seated near one end of the desk which ran across the room opposite the door. Seated at the opposite end was an undersized man with a face on him such as I had never seen. He was evidently one of the "familiars" or followers — the usually unseen "shadows" and protectors — with whom money and other kings have, in all times, been obliged to surround themselves. His face was of an exaggerated Hebrew type, his nose an eagle's beak, the eyes prominent, large, black, and lustrous, with very arching brows — the whole expressive of a diabolical cunning which could only belong to a Faust and a Mephistopheles combined. His one rapid penetrating glance at me as I entered the door, evidently satisfied him that it would be safe to let me approach and speak with his master face to face. At the moment, not taking in the object of his presence, without halting I took a chair by the side of Mr. de Rothschild. The wardens stood outside, covertly peering in through the sash which formed the walls of the room, curious to fathom the design of a visit from so great a money-king. The precise object of his visit I do not remember, but I took advantage of the occasion to see whether anything could be done to relieve Noyes and my brother Austin from the probable consequences of their connection with McDonald and myself.

During the interview, I said: "Mr. Rothschild, I believe most other men placed in the same circumstances, would have done much as I have. I was brought up honestly, and the greater part of my life I have been an honest man. I have plunged myself into a gulf of misery and degradation, but mark my words, I shall live to redeem my character, and, if force of will counts for anything, I shall not die until that end is accomplished."

I have worked, suffered, and *lived* through fifteen years, the resolve then expressed being a beacon light — a light which for long years, though shining brightly, appeared very dim from its vast distance away, and at times it seemed to my wavering eyes to flicker and become extinguished, leaving me in the darkness of despair. Having been protected from birth against every rough wind, Mr. Alfred de Rothschild could see nothing in me worth saving, and the future will decide if he was right.

O ye mighty of the earth! who are yourselves living in luxury — even all who are going through life untroubled by unending struggles for existence — continue unobserving, thoughtless, and blind to the great ocean of misery ever ebbing and flowing beneath the placid surface of society, until the billows of socialism or anarchy suddenly overwhelm all in a common ruin!

A few days later the Lord Mayor Waterlow entered my cell alone. I had already been before him several times at the Mansion House. I do not remember what induced him to make the visit in question, unless to see for himself how I was standing the terrible ordeal, or to judge if I was the desperado I had been represented. At all events, his manner was very affable, and he appeared much interested in the conversation until, as we were standing face to face, I put my hand to my breast pocket to get a letter or paper to illustrate something I had been saying. Seeing the movement of my hand, he suddenly stepped sidewise, out of the cell door. Why he did so flashed through my mind instantly, and I was so shocked that I should be taken for an assassin that I could not continue the conversation.

Whether he went and reported me as having an intention to assassinate him, I know not; but the circumstance led me to think, "If that is their idea of my personal character, what kind of a chance do I stand for an unprejudiced trial?" In the subsequent trial Justice Archibald ruled against us in every objection made by our counselors, and granted every objection or request of the prosecution. But that Imperial Power, the Bank of England, was against us.

On another day the Lord Mayor was doing the honors of the city to the Russian Prince Imperial, the present Emperor. He brought him to my cell accompanied by a retinue of aristocrats, of course the class for whom the world and all it contains was created—I mean its pleasures and the *dolce far niente*, not its pains and labors.

I presume the Lord Mayor wished him to see me as an example of one of the products of modern financial civilization. The retinue remained gazing through the door at me, while the Prince stepped inside preceded by the Lord Mayor Waterlow, who put the "animal" through his paces, no doubt much to the Prince's edification.

The Prince was condescendingly gracious enough to ask me some questions in perfect English, but really, though a wretched prisoner, I could get up no feeling of gratification at his notice beyond what I should have felt at the notice of any gentleman of education and refinement, and such an one the Prince surely was. I think I am entitled to call him an old friend, and to visit him at my earliest convenience in St. Petersburg.

CHAPTER XV.

HELD FOR TRIAL — THE FATAL "NOT GUILTY" — A "TIMES" EDITORIAL — NOYES'S LETTER TO HIS BROTHER READ IN COURT — A TOUCHING SCENE — DEATH OF DETECTIVE M'KELVIE, WHO SECURED MY ARREST IN EDINBURGH — THE LORDS STIRRED UP.

ON the 2d of July, 1873, occurred the last of the twenty-three preliminary examinations before the Lord Mayor Waterlow. It was, all together, an ordeal which I trust no young man who reads this book will ever be called upon to endure. Pilloried in the dock day after day, exposed to the gaze of unsympathetic and curious crowds of people, who coldly speculated as to the result of the trial, and endeavored to penetrate, by dint of staring, through the cloak of impassibility with which the prisoner attempts to hide his real feelings. When the Lord Mayor at last announced that we were to be held for trial, the knowledge that I should remain undisturbed for the month or more before it could take place seemed like a respite.

I had made up my mind to plead guilty, believing that by doing so I should give the others a chance of escape, as their advocates could throw the *onus* on me. I had ascertained that we should be taken to plead to the indictments before Judge Chambers, and was assured by the experienced prison warders that if I pleaded guilty he would not give me more than seven years. But such a course on my part would have spoiled the "big case" which the Bank agents had spent so much time and money in getting up in order to let our fate be a warning to all who dared think of meddling with British money-bags. I believe, and always shall until assured to the contrary by Mr. Freshfield, that these latter had a potent "influence" in causing Solicitor Howell to oppose my plan of pleading guilty, but as what he could say had no effect on my decision, he doubtless instructed my barrister, Mr. Besley, in whom I placed confidence, to advise me not to carry out my intention. Accordingly on Tuesday, the 12th of August, we were taken before Judge Chambers, and when I in my turn stood up to plead, Mr. Besley stepped up to the dock and said to me, in a low tone of voice:

"I hope you are not going to plead guilty?"

Such a remark from such a source, at that moment, staggered me; the clerk of the court was waiting my reply, and I blurted out the fatal words, "Not guilty"—words which cost me the possibility, nay, the probability, that I should never again see the outside of prison walls. Does it stand to reason that a gentleman like Mr. Besley would have caused me to do such a thing unless Solicitor Howell had instructed him to that effect, when even I could see that it was a foregone conclusion that I was to be convicted? I only mention these things to show that however cleverly a man may arrange his rascalities, "something" will happen by which in the end he meets his just deserts.

As a proof of this, in my own case, I will now give an account of the trial, which I have procured from an authentic source, and which will doubtless prove of interest to many outside of the legal profession.

I shall intersperse some criticisms and explanations—not, however, in the way of exculpations, but to show where prosecutors and witnesses made mistakes in facts, identifications, etc. I first introduce the account of the trial by the following editorial from the London *Times* of August 13, 1873:

THE BANK FORGERIES.

Monday next has been fixed for the trial of George Bidwell, Austin   George McDonald, and Edwin Noyes, the four Americans who stand charged with the gigantic forgeries on the Government and Company of the Bank of England. The prisoners will be arraigned before Mr. Justice Archibald, at the Central Criminal Court, and the trial will probably last the whole week. Meanwhile, the voluminous and circumstantial depositions taken before the Lord Mayor at the Justice Room of the Mansion House by Mr. Oke, the Chief Clerk, have been printed for the convenience of the presiding judge and of the counsel on both sides. They extend over 242 folio pages, including the oral and documentary evidence, and make of themselves a thick volume, together with an elaborate index for ready reference. Within living memory there has been no such case for length and importance heard before any Lord Mayor of London in its preliminary stage, nor one which excited a greater amount of public interest from first to last. The Overend-Gurney prosecution is the only one in late years which at all approaches it in those respects, but in that the printed depositions only extended over 164 folio pages, or much less than those in the Bank Case, in which as many as 108 witnesses gave evidence before the Lord Mayor, and the preliminary examinations — twenty-three in number from first to last — lasted from the first of March until the 2d of July, exclusive of the time spent in remands.

Chapter XVI.

REPORT OF THE TRIAL AT THE "OLD BAILEY"—FIRST DAY, MONDAY, AUGUST 18, 1873—THE LEGAL TALENT ENGAGED—ARGUMENTS FOR AND AGAINST POSTPONEMENT—TRIAL MUST PROCEED—THE JURY—MR. GIFFORD, Q. C., OPENS THE CASE FOR THE PROSECUTION—HE OUTLINES THE PLOT—GIVES A SYNOPSIS OF FINANCIAL TRANSACTIONS—AUSTIN'S LETTER TO MAC—MY OWN LETTER TO MAC—"A HELL'S CHASE AND NO MISTAKE"—ADJOURNED FOR LUNCHEON.

ON the opening of the August sessions of the Central Criminal Court, this morning at eleven o'clock, the four Americans, George Bidwell, forty years of age, merchant—George McDonald, twenty-eight years of age, described as a clerk—Austin   twenty-five years of age, described as merchant's clerk—and Edwin Noyes   twenty-eight years of age, called a clerk—were put upon their trial before Mr. Justice Archibald, for the forgeries on the Governor and Company of the Bank of England. The court was much crowded from the beginning, and continued so throughout the day. Alderman Sir Robert Carden, representing the Lord Mayor, Mr. Alderman Finis, Mr. Alderman Besley, Mr. Alderman Lawrence, M. P., Mr. Alderman Whetham, and Mr. Alderman Ellis, as commissioners of the court, occupied seats upon the bench, as did also Alderman Sheriff White.

Sheriff Sir Frederick Perkins, Mr. Under-Sheriff Hewitt, and Mr. Under-Sheriff Crosley, Mr. R. B. Green, Mr. R. W. Crawford, M. P., Governor of the Bank, Mr. Lyall, Deputy Governor, and Mr. Alfred de Rothschild, were present. The

NOTE—I have caused certain portions of the following eight chapters, which contain an account of the trial, to be printed in italics, and it is to these, in general, that my interspersed comments refer.— G. B.

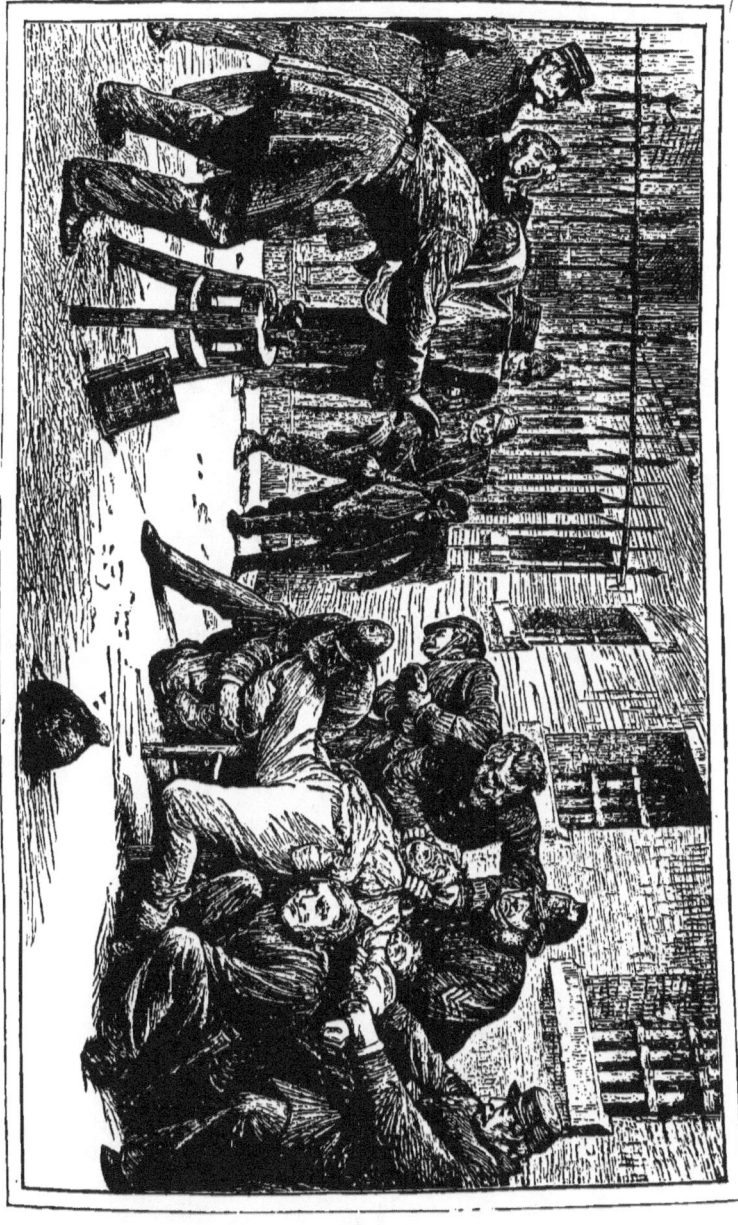

A NEWGATE SCENE.—DON'T WANT HIS PICTURE TAKEN.

members of the bar mustered in force, and the reserved seats were chiefly occupied by ladies. Mr. Hardinge Giffard, Q. C., Mr. Watkin Williams, Q. C., Mr. Poland, Mr. H. D. Green, Mr. J. H. Crawford (instructed by Messrs. Freshfield, the solicitors of the Bank) appeared as counsel for the prosecution.

The prisoner George Bidwell was defended by Mr. Powell, Q. C., and Mr. Besley; Austin by Mr. McIntyre, Q. C., and Mr. Moody (all instructed by Mr. Howell, solicitor); George McDonald, by Mr. Metcalf, Q. C., and Mr. Straight (instructed by Messrs. Wontner, solicitors), and Edwin Noyes by Mr. Ribton and Mr. Hollings (instructed by Mr. Howell).

R. W. CRAWFORD, M.P., GOVERNOR.

Mr. Powell, Q. C., addressing the judge, said he was instructed on the part of his client, George Bidwell, to apply to the court for a further postponement of the trial. There were no fewer than sixteen indictments against the prisoners, charging them with offenses of the gravest magnitude. The evidence was most voluminous and very complicated, and the preliminary inquiry before the Lord Mayor lasted from the 1st of March, when Noyes was arrested, until the 2d of July, when they were all committed for trial. On the 7th of August the prisoners were served with a notice by the Bank solicitor, to the effect that no fewer than ninety-three additional witnesses, whose names they gave, and "divers other persons" might possibly be called upon the part of the prosecution. Except in one or two cases, the prisoners were kept in the dark as to the nature of the evidence the new witnesses would give, and it was therefore impossible, without some investigation, to be prepared with a reply to it. Those witnesses, it was stated, generally would be called to speak of banking or bill transactions with one or other of the prisoners abroad, or to produce letters written by them, and he need hardly say that these matters might, and doubtless would have an important bearing on the case. The prisoners had not had time to inquire into the evidence about to be given, or to instruct counsel with reference to it, and he submitted that it was only fair to them, under the circumstances, that a further adjournment should be granted.

GEORGE LYALL, DEPUTY GOVERNOR.

Assuming that the new witnesses would simply corroborate others already examined, the necessity for inquiry on the part of the prisoners was still very urgent, inasmuch as the production of such a mass of additional evidence was almost an admission that the depositions already taken failed in certain particulars or points that might be of importance to them. Looking at the fact that many of the witnesses lived on the Continent, and that only ten days' notice had been given to the prisoners by the prosecution, he urged that it would be taking the accused, who were foreigners, at a very great disadvantage if the trial was hurried on at that moment, and that there would be a serious risk, and that justice would not be done them. He added that the application was not made with any view to unnecessary delay.

Mr. McIntyre, Q. C., supported the application on behalf of Austin observing that if the prosecution had, prior the last adjournment, formed an intention to call the new witnesses, they should, in fairness to the prisoners, have given them notice six weeks since. If, on the other hand, the existence of ninety-three witnesses had been discovered, or any necessity for calling them had transpired since that adjournment, the prisoners were certainly entitled, on every principle of justice, to an opportunity of defending themselves on the new points about to be raised. It was unfair to the prisoners to expect them to meet allegations which were not gone into before the committing magistrate, and of the substance of which they were as yet unaware.

Mr. Metcalf, Q. C., made a similar appeal on the part of George McDonald, urging that the case for the prosecution had been doubled in extent since it left the Mansion House, that many new heads of evidence were about to be opened, and that it had been impossible, during the nine or ten days since the notice had been served, to make any inquiry as to the statements the witnesses would be called upon to give.

Mr. Ribton, on behalf of Noyes, said applications for postponement were very frequently made in that court, and were hardly ever opposed or rejected, especially when they came from persons in the dock. As for his own client (Noyes) his case differed materially from that of the others, and it was very unfair to be informed, at the last moment, that it was proposed to show the previous acquaintanceship of all the prisoners in America, seeing that the accused men had no opportunity of inquiring into the character of the persons who were about to give such evidence. He should have thought that the Bank authorities, acting, as it might be supposed they did, solely in public interest, and possessing inexhaustible resources, would have been ready to consent to such a reasonable application.

Mr. Giffard, Q. C., for the prosecution, strongly resisted the applications. He pointed out that, although the case had lasted upwards of four months at the police court, the delay, if any, had arisen from the fact that Austin had to be brought to this country from Havana, and McDonald from New York. The charge was in itself a very simple one, but the tracing of the various bills was somewhat complicated.

There was no legal obligation on the part of the prosecution to give the accused notice of fresh evidence, but such notice was invariably given out of mere fairness. It was quite impossible for any one at a preliminary inquiry to say what new witnesses might be forthcoming between the date of the committal and the trial, so it had been found in this instance. Of the new witnesses referred to, forty were bank clerks and others, who would, if necessary, give more formal proof on matters already investigated, and some of the rest would speak to the purchase by the prisoners of genuine bills at various places on the Continent, which were afterwards used as models for forged bills.

There had been great difficulty in getting some of the witnesses from America and the Continent, and if the trial were again postponed there would certainly be a failure of justice. The application by the prisoners was simply made with a view to delay, and in the hope that some of the material witnesses would be wanting on a future occasion. He submitted with confidence that no cause for the delay had been shown.

Mr. Justice Archibald, having taken time to consider his answer, said he had carefully weighed all that had been urged on the part of the prisoners, and he had come to the decision to refuse the application, having a very clear opinion that no injustice to the prisoners would ensue if the trial proceeded without delay.

A jury having been empaneled and sworn, Mr. Avery, the clerk of arraigns, addressing them, said the prisoners were severally indicted for forging and uttering on the 17th of January last, a bill of exchange for £1,000, purporting to be drawn by H. C. Streeter of Valparaiso, and accepted by the London and Westminster Bank, with the intent to defraud the Governor and Company of the Bank of England. In other counts he said they were charged in like manner with other forgeries, variously stated.

Mr. Giffard then proceeded to open the case for the prosecution. The prisoners he said were indicted for forging and uttering a bill of exchange for £1,000, but that in reality formed but a very small part of the scheme, or fraud, which it would be his duty to lay before the jury.

The charge against them was in substance that of uttering ninety-four bills of exchange, all of which were forged, and the effect of which was to obtain from the Bank of England very large sums of money. The jury would therefore at once perceive that they had to try a charge of fraud for which they might seek in vain a parallel in the criminal annals of the country. Such an enterprise, as might well be imagined, involved very considerable difficulties, but that all those difficulties were long contemplated the jury in the end would probably have no doubt, and as little doubt that they were surmounted with such consummate art as to produce a feeling of regret that the prisoners had not employed their talents to legitimate purposes in the ordinary business of life. Moreover, that scheme of fraud, but for one of those accidents which had come to be embodied in various shapes in the common proverbs of the country, was all but successful in the result. The jury would, therefore, perceive the class of men they had to try, how deeply they had laid their plot, and with what consummate skill they carried it into execution. The prisoners George Bidwell, Austin and George McDonald, as would be proved, came to this country in the spring of last year *to set on foot an original scheme of fraud. The first difficulty with which they had to contend was to procure an introduction to the Bank of England or to some first-rate bank, and at which they might discount bills.* Austin Bidwell *had been accustomed to deal* with a respectable firm of tailors named Green, in Saville Row, and one day in May, 1872, having made a purchase from them, he stated that he was about to depart for Ireland, and that he had a large sum of money in his possession, of which he wished them to take charge in his absence. Mr. Green declined the responsibility, and suggested that he (Bidwell) should place the sum *on deposit at the Western Branch of the Bank of England*, where his firm banked. The suggestion was adopted, and he and Bidwell walked together to the bank, where they saw Mr. Fenwick, the sub-manager. Bidwell gave the name of Frederick Albert Warren, and having deposited the money, *he innocently inquired if, supposing he had any further sum to pay in, he need trouble Mr. Green who had introduced him, to come with him for that purpose. He was told that their account was henceforth his own and that he could pay in the money direct.* The amount paid in upon that day was £1,200, and the prisoner subsequently deposited a further sum of £1,000. After that the account was allowed to rest until September, when the prisoner called at the bank, and requested Col. Francis, the manager, to sell for him £8,000 worth of Portuguese three per cent. bonds. This was assented to, and the prisoner drew £2,000 on account. During that interview with the manager the prisoner stated, casually, that he was an American contractor, or agent, charged with the introduction on an extensive scale of Pullman's sleeping-cars into this country, and upon the Continent, that he was about to build them at Birmingham, and that he hoped to have some of them running for the impending exhibition at Vienna. *The prisoner's account at the bank went on smoothly and regularly* and no particular attention was paid to it by the authorities. (See page   et seq.)

It would be found that having obtained the all-important introduction to the Bank, and having overcome the preliminary difficulties, the next point with the persons concocting this gigantic fraud was to know what to forge. *During September and October, therefore, they were actively engaged in various capitals and cities of Europe in making inquiries as to the solvency and status of various large commercial houses, and the amount of respect their bills were likely to command in London, and to acquaint themselves generally with the ordinary course of transactions there and in this country,* so that they might be perfectly armed at every step of their way. [I did the whole of that work.—G. B.] About this time two of the prisoners became ill, and on the 5th of October Austin wrote a letter to McDonald containing this passage: " G. (meaning his brother) has just telegraphed if we shall not wait until you are completely restored, and in answering it I trust that you will not be governed by any thought that we want you to go on at once. Far from it; the first consideration is your health, and if necessary we will postpone business until Christmas, and if you require rest for ten days or more, for heaven's sake take it; it might be highly dangerous for you to stir about. Then, we have a good capital, and when ready can largely increase it on short order. Above all things, if your health requires it let us wait, for business cannot be injured by delay; it is only a matter of resting for that time."

[In establishing his theory that the fraud was a long-contemplated one, Mr. Giffard made an effective usage of the 'letter from my brother; but it will be seen by reference to page   that the first inception of the "scheme" was not till on or about the 1st of November, nearly a month later than the date of my brother's letter. The telegram referred to as from G. is one I sent from Amsterdam while prospecting in search of an opening for a "speculation" somewhere on the Continent.—G. B.]

Mr. Giffard continued: The scheme had in consequence to be postponed, and the prisoners did not in fact commence active operations until Christmas. Between November and January George Bidwell, under the name of Gilbert, procured a large number of bills, which not only formed the model of the various forged ones, but, being paid into the Bank of England and duly honored, served to establish the mercantile credit of Warren there. It would be found also that either McDonald or Austin   giving the name of Warren, went to Rotterdam and applied to a Mr. DeWael, a merchant there, for a draft on the London and Westminster Bank.

He was told that there was only one person at Rotterdam entitled to draw on that bank, and that he charged highly for it. Warren replied that he did not mind the expense, but that he must have the bill on that particular bank, and he accordingly left £622 with Mr. DeWael to purchase a draft, giving as his address in London the Golden Cross Hotel. [Another case of mistaken identification. I transacted that business with Mr. DeWael.—G. B.] Bills to the amount of between £4,000 and £5,000 were obtained by the prisoners during these three months, their evident object being to get first-class paper and induce the bank to discount their bills. On the 29th of November Austin went to Col. Francis, and producing two genuine bills for £500, each accepted by Messrs. Suse & Sibeth, an eminent firm in London, asked him if he would discount paper of that sort. [Bills purchased for me by Mr. Pinto in Amsterdam. —G. B.] The manager promised to make inquiries, and finding they were first-class bills he discounted them. The prisoners having thus, with consummate skill and at one stroke, obtained credit with the Bank of England and the models for the forged bills which were to come, next provided for the distribution of the plunder and their means of escape. It was manifestly impossible that the money could be withdrawn in gold alone, and the prisoners no doubt felt that to receive it in bank notes was the most dangerous course they could adopt.

The difficulty was surmounted by the opening by Austin [By my direction.—G. B.], in the name of Charles Johnson Horton, of an account at the Continental Bank in Lombard Street, into which he could pay the money received at the Western Branch and then draw it out again in a different shape. The account was opened on the 2d of December [After McDonald's "great discovery." See page —G. B.], which day also introduced the jury to the fourth prisoner, Edwin Noyes. He was in New York at the time, and the prisoner, George Bidwell, telegraphed to him in effect to come over to this country on the next steamer without fail.

The jury would probably find in the end that a fourth person had become absolutely necessary to the successful execution of the scheme.

George Bidwell and McDonald had by that time become deeply concerned in it, and were thenceforward to be kept in the background. It was necessary, therefore, that some person who up to that time had been a stranger to the transaction should be introduced, and Noyes was selected for the purpose. On the 17th of December he arrived in England, and apparently without any luggage. *In the previous August McDonald had been in communication with him by telegraph*, and the jury would see eventually whether Noyes was the stranger he affected to be. He arrived in London on the 17th of December, and on the 18th or 19th he was dressed up for the part he had to play, and various precautions were taken to conceal his identity. It was absolutely astonishing to note in the progress of the fraud *the number of aliases* [see page] the prisoners, with the exception of Noyes, had occasion to assume. The jury would have occasion, as the trial proceeded, to note the intimacy which existed between Noyes and the other prisoners, and would find that up to the 11th of January, from his first coming to this country, he was in the closest relations with them. On Christmas day there was a dinner party at which all the four prisoners were present. That was the state of things up to the end of January. During December neither of the prisoners, George Bidwell nor McDonald, had been idle. Austin   was the person to open the account at the Western Branch of the Bank of England, and *part of the plot* was that he should be out of the country before the first forged bill was uttered. [See page] The other prisoners, as to whom the Bank could have no information, were not only the persons who procured the models for the forged bills, but who actually forged them.

The jury would find George Bidwell going to various engravers for that purpose. He [Mr. Giffard] would not describe each individual transaction of that kind; it would suffice to say that whenever the prisoners obtained a genuine bill, they had the means in their own hands of counterfeiting it, by having recourse to engravers, and that by various expedients suspicion was disarmed. One of the forged bills purported to be accepted at the London and Westminster Bank, and a stamp was fabricated so as to imitate that by which the genuine acceptance of the bank was accustomed to be made.

It was necessary to protect the man Noyes, who was acting as Horton's clerk, and it was therefore clearly impossible that he could have any connection with Warren's account at the Bank of England. An extremely cunning device was then arranged. Austin   explained to Col. Francis that his workshops were being constructed at Birmingham, and that his presence there was necessary; and he stated that his bills, instead of being presented personally as hitherto, would be sent through the post in registered letters. *The first letter was dated the 30th of December* [two months after the first inception of the fraud. See Chapter   —G. B.], and contained ten genuine bills for £4,807 3s. 6d., all of which were discounted and subsequently honored. On the 5th of January an advertisement was inserted in the newspapers, by Noyes, to the effect that a gentleman of active business habits, and with a small capital of £300, required a situation as clerk or partner, and answers were to be addressed to him at Durant's Hotel, where he was then staying. A great many answers were received, and McDonald called at the hotel personally. [Another mistake in identification, as it was not McDonald who called at the hotel.—G. B.] After he left, Noyes told the waiter that he was his future master, and that he had deposited £300 with him as a guarantee for his good conduct. On the 11th of January a formal agreement was entered into between Charles Johnson Horton of London Bridge, a Pullman car manufacturer, and Edwin Noyes of Durant's Hotel, merchant's clerk, whereby Noyes agreed to serve the former as clerk and manager, at a salary of £150, the latter depositing a sum of £300 as security for the due performance of his duties and honesty, said sum to be returned without interest on his leaving. The agreement was witnessed by Mr. Howell, a solicitor in Cheapside, who was now defending the prisoners, and it was found in Noyes's possession on his arrest. It was evidently intended to shield him when the fraud was discovered, and when all the other parties had made their escape. Up to this time very good bills had been sent up to the Bank for discount, but before the forgeries commenced a grand *coup* was determined upon. Accordingly Austin early in January, obtained a considerable quantity of foreign money and left London for Paris. On his way there he was considerably injured by an accident on the Great Northern Railway of France, but he turned the accident to account by introducing himself to Messrs. Rothschild, who had a close financial connection with the Railway Company. He induced them, against their ordinary practice, to sell him a bill of £4,500, and with this he returned immediately to London. [I purchased all this foreign money in London, and sent Austin to purchase a bill from Rothschild, the railway accident having nothing to do with it, beyond influencing the bankers to accede to his request.— G. B.] He had an interview with Col. Francis, and in the course of it he complained in some degree that his bills were being unnecessarily watched, inasmuch as all which he had presented were of the highest possible character. [Complained that his bills were being unnecessarily watched! If that statement is well founded, it should have been quite sufficient to arouse suspicion and cause inquiry — but no forger would be so stupid.— G. B.] He then threw down the bill of Messrs. Rothschild, saying he supposed that would be good enough for the Bank. It not being advisable for him to confess that he had left Birmingham and obtained the bill in Paris, he stated that the injuries from which he was suffering had been caused by a fall from his horse. He also stated that his workshops at Birmingham were full of new sleeping-cars, and that he expected his transactions to be very large in the course of the ensuing month.

The scheme involved not only the protection of the conspirators but the safety of the plunder, and accordingly it was, beyond all doubt, arranged that he should be on his way out of the country before the first forged bill reached the Western Branch of the Bank of England. It had been suggested at the preliminary examination before the Lord Mayor that because Austin   was out of the country he was not amenable for this offense. That was neither sound law nor common sense. There was a very old legal maxim that a man who did an act by another, did it by himself. The prisoner, Austin   might have done what he did either at Rome or Kamtschatka, but he would be equally responsible, notwithstanding.

[The Northern Railway accident, while on his journey to Paris, and his engagement, caused Austin to give up connection with the partially prepared fraud, and he was absent on his "wedding journey." See Chapter   for particulars. But Mr. Giffard's assertion is "good law and common sense," and should be a warning to any who contemplate perpetrating crime by proxy.—G. B.]

On the 22d of January, 1873, in a letter signed by Warren, dated on the 21st, came the first batch of forged bills to the Western Branch. That was the first experiment, and if it passed muster the scheme was successful. Austin would then appear to have fled, and Noyes could set up the defense that he had merely acted as his clerk. The scheme was successful; *the bills had been engraved by skilled artisans* and had passed muster; the thing was done; and having got the first forged bills discounted, the next step was to operate on the account previously opened to get the plunder, and to escape. But having obtained so much money, how were they to deal with it?

Notes could be traced. The scheme contrived was as artful as the rest of the fraud. Anybody presenting banknotes at the Bank of England had a right to demand gold in exchange, but it might not be so generally known that the converse proceeding was equally easy, viz., that a person tendering gold at the Bank of England could receive its equivalent in notes. The device adopted in this case was this:

One of the prisoners went to the bank with notes and obtained gold for them. Another of them went on the same day and obtained notes for the gold; so that unless it could be shown that the two prisoners so acting were associated in a common design the connection between the fraud and the property actually obtained by it was broken. That process was repeated to such an extent that between the 21st of January and the 28th of February, the notes changed into gold by Noyes amounted to no less than £23,650, and the gold exchanged for other notes by McDonald to £16,950. There was thus a large balance in favor of the amount in gold, but both it and the notes were afterwards expended in the purchase of United States bonds. Austin left this country in the middle of January, and was married to an English lady in Paris. And he seemed to have gone about France and Germany selling the bonds which had been bought in London and buying others with a view further to destroy all trace of the proceeds of the fraud. [If he did so it was without my knowledge.— G. B.] About this time, also, Noyes sent out £1,000 to some relations in America, and it was, therefore, idle to pretend that he was merely the innocent clerk of the other men.

The business up to this point was eminently successful, and the diligence of the prisoners in the previous December was not without its reward.

From the 28th of January every bill which was sent to the bank was a forgery and had been fabricated on the model of the genuine bills, Messrs. Rothschild included, which had previously been discounted.

The first batch amounted to £4,250 and was discounted on the 21st of January, and then came the following in quick succession. On the 4th of February, £11,072; 10th of February, £4,642; 13th of February, £14,696; 20th of February, £14,686; 24th of February, £19,253; and 28th of February, £24,265. The prisoner gave no address at Birmingham, but he explained that as he was staying with a friend a short distance out of town he should like his letters addressed to the post-office there, and that was accordingly done. On the 1st of February, McDonald deposited £1,200, part of the proceeds of the forgeries, with Messrs. J. S. Morgan & Co., the American bankers, and drew it out again on the twenty-first of that month. One of the bank-notes in which the sum was paid had been traced into the possession of George Bidwell, and another was found upon Noyes at the time of his arrest. In this transaction, therefore, the four prisoners were concerned. The first forged bill would become due on the 25th of March, and it was so arranged that during the whole of the time the forged bills were pouring into the bank the genuine bills previously discounted were becoming due and being paid.

While the prisoners were making their arrangements to escape, the forgeries were discovered in the most accidental way. Two bills for £1,000 each, purported to be accepted by Mr. W. Blydenstein of Great St. Helens, had been made payable at sight, but curiously enough the date had been omitted, and the bank authorities suspecting nothing wrong, sent a clerk on to Mr. Blydenstein's office to get the omission supplied. The moment the bills were seen the forgery was discovered, and the scheme of the prisoners was at an end. The bank found that Warren had been operating upon Horton's account at the Continental Bank, and by a mere accident the chief cashier of the bank happened to be making inquiries there when the prisoner Noyes entered. He was at once pointed out and given into custody, and it was found that on the same day he had purchased £26,000 worth of American bonds, and had cashed a check of Horton's for £5,000. What was his conduct when arrested? He knew that both McDonald and George Bidwell were within the grasp of the law, but he made no disclosure, and he merely gave an address at Durant's Hotel, where he had not slept for a fortnight. He thus allowed his confederates time to collect the plunder, then lying at his and their lodgings, and to send it to other countries, the result being that some part of it was still unrecovered. A day or two later Bidwell and McDonald went to a hotel at St. Leonard's, and ordering a large fire to be prepared, they, as the prosecution alleged, destroyed all the plant used in the course of this scheme. [This is an error, it having been destroyed at Mac's lodgings in London, as previously stated. — G. B.] On the same occasion they sent to New York £50,000 worth of American bonds in a trunk addressed to Major George Matthews, which has since been seized by the police. In the rooms occupied by McDonald in St. James Street, blotting-paper was found bearing impressions of the writing in some letters addressed to Austin   at New York, and of the stamps and endorsements of the forged bills, and a London directory was also discovered from which a list of engravers was cut. Mr. Giffard then went in detail into the circumstances of the prisoner George Bidwell's escape into Ireland, of his ultimate arrest in Edinburgh, and read a passage in a letter addressed by him to George McDonald, as follows:

Your friend has had a series of most extraordinary adventures since you saw him. A hell's chase and no mistake. His nerve has stood him through two taps on the shoulder, and four encounters with detectives. He has been a Fenian, a priest, a professor, a Frenchman, a German, a Russian who could speak only "veree leetle Engles, mais un peu de Français et Allemand," and a deaf and dumb man with a slate and pencil,— all in the space of a week.

The learned counsel also described the prisoner's unsuccessful efforts to get rid of some of the witnesses in the case, and his attempts to make sure that the property reached America safely. He also stated that George Bidwell had assumed sixteen different *aliases*.

That he said was the case for the prosecution, and the jury would say by their verdict when they heard the evidence whether it was possible to entertain the smallest doubt that each and all of the prisoners combined together in carrying out their gigantic scheme, and having as they thought destroyed all traces of the proceeds, sought to betake themselves to another country, and there enjoy their ill-gotten gains.

It being now five o'clock, and Mr. Giffard having finished his opening statement, after speaking upwards of three hours, the trial was adjourned until next morning, and the jury were escorted by a sworn officer of the court to the Cannon Street Terminus Hotel, to pass the night without separating.

About one o'clock each day the court adjourned for luncheon. The illustrations will give an idea of what kind of a time the lawyers were having, while we poor wretches were put beneath into a large vaulted cell in the basement of the Old Bailey. Some food was brought in from a restaurant, but none of us were in circumstances to feel jolly over our dinner. Neither of us could avoid the thought that a very slight turn in the tide of affairs, at some period of his life, might have made him one of the laughing lunchers above, instead of a *miserable* below stairs.

BENEATH OLD BAILEY COURT ROOM—COURT ADJOURNED FOR LUNCH.

Chapter XVII.

THE TRIAL CONTINUED—SECOND DAY, TUESDAY, AUGUST 19TH—COL. PEREGRINE MADGWICK FRANCIS, MANAGER OF THE WESTERN BRANCH OF THE BANK OF ENGLAND—COMMERCIAL CORRESPONDENCE—A ROTHSCHILD'S SIGNATURE.

AT the opening of the court at ten o'clock, the trial begun the day before continued to excite much interest.

Col Francis said: On the 22d of January I received the registered letter produced from Warren, and three bills enclosed with a memorandum. The amount was for £4,250, and the bills were endorsed by him. The letter was as follows:

BIRMINGHAM, January 21, 1873.

DEAR SIR:—I hand you herewith, as per enclosed memorandum, bills for discount, the proceeds of which please place to my credit.

I remain, dear sir, Yours very truly,
F. A. WARREN.
To Col. P. M. FRANCIS,
Manager Western Branch of the Bank of England.

[Above and following letters were written by me, Warren not being in England.— G. B.]

Mr. Giffard, interposing, said: We propose to read the first bill now, as that is a subject of indictment. Mr. Avery, the clerk of the arraigns, said the bill was one for £1,000, purporting to be drawn by H. C. Streeter, and accepted, payable three months after date, by the London and Westminster Bank. This acceptance was in the names of Mr. H. F. Billinghurst, the sub-country manager, and Mr. W. H. Nichols, signing on behalf of the secretary. Col. Francis, resuming, said: Those three acceptances are similar to some of the general acceptances given on the 30th of December. They were all discounted, and the account credited with the amount. They became due on the 31st of March, the 3d of April, and the 13th of April. They were presented in due course, and returned as forged.

On the 25th of January I received the registered letter and memorandum produced from Birmingham, with the eight bills mentioned in the memorandum. The letter was as follows:

BIRMINGHAM, January 24, 1873..
COL. P. M. FRANCIS, Manager Western Branch Bank of England:
DEAR SIR, — Enclosed I hand you bills for discount, as per enclosed memorandum, and which please have placed to my credit on receipt. The reduction in Bank rate came quite opportunely for my wants. I am, dear sir,
Yours very truly,   F. A. WARREN.

I do not think the signature to the letter is Warren's. It is an imitation of it, but I took it at the time to be in his handwriting. I also took the endorsements to the bills to be in his handwriting. There were eight bills, and they were discounted by me and placed to Warren's credit.

Mr. McIntyre, interposing, objected to the admissibility of this evidence, on the ground that it was not proved to be in Warren's handwriting. Mr. Justice Archibald overruled the objection, saying it would be a matter on which to address the jury when the proper time arrived. Mr. McIntyre submitted there was no evidence of authority. The judge said he would take a note of the objection. Witness, resuming, said: The amount of the bills in question was £9,350, and that sum was placed to the credit of the account, on the 25th. Of the eight bills, two purported to be accepted by Messrs. N. M. de Rothschild & Sons, two by Mr. B. W. Blydenstein, one by the Anglo-Austrian Bank, one by Suse & Sibeth, one by the London and Westminster Bank.

NINE BANKERS TESTIFY. 169

Mr. Alfred Charles de Rothschild was called and examined N. M. de Rothschild & Sons. Being shown eight bills purporting to be those of his firm, he said the acceptance was not in the handwriting of any member of it. The stamp across the bill, he said, was an imitation of the stamp they used for acceptances, and was not genuine. Shown a genuine bill of their firm for £4,500, he said it was in the handwriting of Sir Anthony de Rothschild.

Being cross-examined by Mr. McIntyre, witness said that the bill was drawn by their house in London on their Paris house. He added that the acceptance of the forged bill was exactly that which the firm used.

By Mr. Giffard: The signature to the forged bills produced purported to be that of Sir Anthony de Rothschild, but in every case it was a forgery. There was a certain amount of imitation of the signatures, and some might think it good, but he did not.

Mr. John Rudolph Lorent, manager of the Bank of Belgium and Holland — Mr. Herman Gwinner, manager of the International Bank of Hamburg and London — Mr. Charles John Sibeth, of the firm of Messrs. Suse & Sibeth, 35 Lime Street — Mr. Francis Hamilton, of the firm of Messrs. Brown, Shipley & Co. — Mr. Chas. Lloyd Norman, of the firm of Messrs. Baring Brothers — Mr. Mayern, clerk in the Russian Bank of Foreign Trade — Mr. J. T. Byng, assistant manager of the Union Bank — Mr. W. H. Trumpler, of the firm of B. W. Blydenstein & Co. — and Mr. W. H. Nichols, of the London and Westminster Bank — were also called, and gave similar evidence as to bills purporting to bear their acceptances. This concluded that class of evidence, and the Court adjourned at four o'clock for the day. Two of the jury were unwell, but the charge being one of felony, the members were not allowed to separate during the progress of the trial, and were taken, as on the previous evening, to the Terminus Hotel, Cannon Street, escorted by an officer of the Court, to spend the night.

Chapter XVIII.

MR. FREDERICK ROBERT RUMSEY PAYS CHECKS OVER THE COUNTER—MR. J. A. C. GOOD DOES LIKEWISE—THE DEFUNCT BANKING HOUSE OF BOWLES BROTHERS—AN AMERICAN GENTLEMAN—THE MANAGER OF THE CONTINENTAL BANK IN THE WITNESS-BOX—BANK OF ENGLAND NOTES EXCHANGED FOR GOLD, AND VICE VERSA—CHECKS CASHED FOR LARGE SUMS, BY THE DOZEN—HEADQUARTERS REMOVED FROM THE TERMINUS HOTEL, LONDON BRIDGE, TO CANNON STREET HOTEL—WARREN CHECKS ON THE WESTERN BRANCH—HORTON BUYS GERMAN MONEY—£1,000 BANK NOTES—TRANSACTIONS WITH JAY COOK, M'CULLOUGH & CO.—EDWARD BRENT, FREDERICK PEARSE, H. W. HUGHES, AND JOSEPH REESE ADAMS, EMPLOYES OF THE BANK OF ENGLAND, TESTIFY—LIGHT WEIGHT SOVEREIGNS.

MR. Frederick Robert Rumsey, a clerk in the Western Branch of the Bank of England, proved from his counter-book that on the 29th of November last he paid over the counter a check of F. A. Warren for £800 in seven £100 notes, and two for £50 each. That was in one check.

Mr. J. A. C. Good, also a clerk in the Western Branch of the Bank of England, proved that on the 2d of December he paid in exchange for a check of Warren for £1,250, twelve bank-notes for £100 each, and £50 in gold.

Mr. John Thomas Stanton, manager of the Continental Bank, 79 Lombard Street, which is also known as Messrs. Hartland & Co., said he saw the prisoners, Noyes and C. J. Horton, at the bank together. On the 2d of Decem-

ber last he first saw Austin He then called at the
bank and opened an account with them. He said that he
had previously had an account with Messrs. Bowles Bros.,
and that he had been fortunate enough to have drawn from
them £7,500 just before their suspension. Having asked
witness what interest would be allowed, it was arranged that
he should open a current account with the Continental Bank.
He opened that account in the name of Charles Johnson
Horton, and signed the signature-book of the bank in that
name, giving as his address the Charing Cross Hotel. Witness understood that he was an American gentleman. The
account was opened by his paying in £1,300 in Bank of England notes, and he filled up a credit slip for that amount.
Witness produced the notes, with the exception of £100
which was changed for the prisoner. [These were the notes
referred to by the last two witnesses.] That was the first
time witness had seen him. Next day the prisoner called
again and paid in £235 10s., in two checks—one of Messrs.
Baring for £50, and the other for £185 10s. in the name of
F. A. Warren, on the Bank of England. Those were credited
to his account. On the 5th of December he paid in a check
for £95 2s., with which his account was credited. On the
same day a check was drawn out by him, signed "C. J. Horton." [Check was for the amount of £1,000.] It was paid
in bank-notes. On the 27th of December witness cashed a
check for him for £100 by £90 in notes and £10 in gold.
On the 30th of December a check of F. A. Warren on the
Bank of England for £1,550 was paid in and credited to his
account. On the 31st of December there was standing to the
credit of Horton's account £1,645 11s. 11d. On the same
day he paid to Horton the sum of £85 in bank-notes in payment of a check of his. On the 9th of January £3,000 was
paid into the account in bank-notes, the credit-slip accompanying the payment being initialed "C. J. H." On the 11th
of January £500 was paid into the same account by Horton,
and the account was credited with the amount. On the same

day £3,933 2s. 10d. was drawn out by, witness presumed, a check of Horton's, for which they gave him French notes for 28,000 francs, and two drafts on Paris — one for 50,000 francs, and the other for 22,000 francs — both drawn on Messrs. Meyer Fils. On the 16th of January £1,250 was cashed over the counter in answer to a check of Horton's. On the 11th a new check-book was supplied to Horton, containing forty-eight checks. On the 16th of January £75 was drawn out by a check of his. On the 18th of January £3,304 16s. 9d. was paid into the account in two checks on the Western Branch of the Bank of England — one for £1,600, and the other for £1,704 16s. 9d. It was not stated upon whom the checks were drawn. On the 21st of January a check of Horton's for £2,000 was cashed, in ten bank-notes of £100 each, and two of £500 each. That was an open check paid over the counter. On the same day a check of Horton's for £807 15s. in favor of Messrs. Jay Cooke, M'Culloch & Co. was paid. On the 22d of January a sum of £3,716 13s. 7d., in two checks — one for £2,300, and the other for £1,416 13s. 7d. — on the Western Branch of the Bank of England, was paid in. On the same day a check of Horton's for £400 was cashed over the counter by two notes of £50 and three of £100. On the 24th of January £2,200 on a check of Horton's was paid, and later in the day a check of his for £45. The larger sum was paid by a check of his on the Union Bank of London, and the smaller check in bank-notes — one of £5, and two of £20.

On the 25th of January, £3,400 was paid in by a check of Warren's on the Western Branch of the Bank of England for that amount. Witness knew the prisoner Noyes. He was introduced to him at their bank by Austin as his clerk. That was about the 18th of January. He said that Noyes was his confidential clerk and that they were to treat him exactly as they treated himself. Witness asked whether Noyes was to be allowed to sign checks. The answer was "By no means," or to that effect. Witness understood that Horton was then going to Birmingham. He did not think he saw Horton after that.

Witness afterwards did business with Noyes in the way of cashing checks and paying in money. On the 25th of January or the day after, he received a letter from Noyes, saying he was to hand the bearer the German money bought for him by C. J. Horton that day. Witness believed that Horton had bought some German money that day which they had not previously had in the bank. It amounted to 2,000 thalers odd, and was given to the bearer, who signed a receipt for it in the name of E. Noyes. Witness, however, sent a clerk from the bank with the messenger to room No. 6, Terminus Hotel, London Bridge, Horton's address. On the 25th of January, a check of Horton's for £1,000 was paid in bank-notes, five of £100, and the rest in foreign money, florins and thalers, amounting to £502 odd. On the 27th of January, a check of Horton's for £451 15s. was paid in favor of Jay Cooke & Co. Next day a check of Horton's for £3,000 was presented and paid over the counter in seventeen £100 notes, five £50 notes, and £1,049 17s. 9d. in Dutch coin. On the 3d of February, £1,000 was paid in to Horton's account, the credit-slip for for which was signed "E. Noyes," in the prisoner's handwriting. That was by a check on the Western Branch of the Bank of England. On February 4th, £3,891 14s. was paid in to the credit of Horton's account by E. Noyes. It consisted of a single check on the Western Branch of the Bank of England. On the same day, a check of Horton's for £1,320 was paid over the counter in six £100 notes, one of £50, one of £10, one of £5, and £654 1s. 9d. in Dutch florins. On February 7th, a check of £3,500 of Horton's was paid over the counter in notes, six of £500 each, and five of £100 each. On February 10th, a check of Horton's for £200 was paid over the counter in notes. On February 13th, £6,250 was paid in to the credit of Horton's account in two checks, one for £4,250, and the other for £2,000, on the Western Branch of the Bank of England, in the name of "F. A. Warren" the credit-slip being signed "E. Noyes." On the same day a check of Horton's for £65 was paid in notes. That sum witness declined to send by a messenger whom Noyes had despatched for it with a letter addressed from the Terminus Hotel, London Bridge. Noyes afterwards called for the money himself, and requested that, in the future, witness would trust the messengers he sent. On February 14th, witness received a letter from Noyes, containing a check of Horton's for £50, which witness cashed at his request, and sent by the bearer to room 6, Terminus Hotel, London Bridge. On February 15th, a check for £332 10s. was paid into the credit of Horton's account. On the same day, he paid a check of Horton's for £4,000 in fourteen bank-notes, two of £1,000, two of £500, and ten of £100. On February 17th, £1,200 was paid in to the credit of Horton's account, in a check of " F. A. Warren " on the Bank of England. On the same day, he cashed a check of Horton's for £2,800 in bank-notes, one for £1,000, two for £500, one for £200, five for £100, and two for £50. On the 20th, he paid a check of Horton's for £1,000 in one note, and that was enclosed in a letter, at the request of Noyes, addressed to Horton at the Cannon Street Hotel, and sent by a messenger. On February 21st, a check of Warren's for £4,500 was paid in to Horton's credit, the slip for which was in Noyes' handwriting. On February 25th, £4,500 was paid partly in bank-notes on a check of Horton's made payable to himself, viz.: four notes of £1,000 each, one of £100, being, said Mr. Poland, one of a batch contained in the envelope produced yesterday by the witness, Mr. Duncan. On February 26th, £2,277 10s. was paid in to the credit of Horton's account, credit-slip for which was signed by Noyes — in two checks, one being a check of Warren's for £2,100, and the other a check of Jay Cooke, M'Culloch & Co.'s for £177 10s. On the 27th of February a check of Horton's for £100 payable to " self or order " was sent, as directed in a letter from Noyes, to C. J. Horton, Room 8, Cannon Street Hotel. Next day a check of Warren's for £6,000 was paid in by Noyes and was payable to Thomas Carter or order. On that occasion Noyes ordered a

very large sum of foreign money to be got ready for him by
the next day, principally in French notes and the rest in
thaler notes. Witness believed the amount of foreign money
he 'ordered was larger than £2,000. On the same occasion,
Noyes received cash for a check of Horton's dated the 28th of
February, for £2,000 in two bank notes of £1,000 each. On
March 1st, Noyes called again, and produced a credit-slip
signed by himself for £2,500, handing in at the same time a
check of Warren's for £2,500 on the Bank of England payable to C. J. Horton. By that time witness had got a portion of foreign money for him, but it was arranged that he
should call for it again later in the day. He called again a
little before one and then produced for payment a check of
Horton's payable to self or order for £5,000. He had to wait
a short time while the check was being collected. Mr. May,
a gentleman connected with the Bank of England, came into
the bank while Noyes was waiting. Upon that witness
pointed him out to Mr. May, who had brought in a policeman
with him, into whose custody Noyes was then given. Witness had not at that time paid the £5,000 check presented by
Noyes.

The witness underwent cross-examination by Mr. McIntyre, Q. C., and Mr. Ribton, but without his evidence in chief
in any material respect being impaired. He said, however,
on every occasion for a considerable time, he dealt with
Noyes, believing him to be Horton's clerk, but after Horton
said he (Noyes) was to be treated with as much respect as
himself, witness thought Noyes was to be treated as somewhat
of a principal. Horton, however, gave witness emphatically to
understand that Noyes was not to sign checks.

Mr. Edward Brent, a clerk in the issue department of the
Bank of England, said he knew the prisoner Noyes as a
person who used to come from time to time to the bank to
exchange notes into gold. On every occasion he asked the
prisoner whether the gold was for home use or for exporta-
tion, and in most cases Noyes said it was for home use; in

the other cases, at a later period, he said it was for Paris. He gave as his address 28 Manchester Square, Durant's Hotel. The total value of the notes he so exchanged was £13,285.

Mr. Frederick Pearse, a clerk in the issue department of the Bank of England, handed in an estimate of the quantity of notes which had been exchanged for gold at the bank.

WEIGHING OFFICE, BANK OF ENGLAND.

Mr. H. W. Hughes, a clerk in the weighing-room of the Bank of England, said he knew the prisoner, McDonald. On the 18th of January he saw that prisoner talking to the principal of the weighing department. The prisoner had brought £6,800 in gold which he wanted to exchange into notes.

Witness found there were twenty-three sovereigns too many, and he told him so. He replied that he was not aware of it. The prisoner gave his name as George McDonald and told him how to spell it, saying he had great difficulty in getting people to spell it correctly. On February 23d, the prisoner called again to exchange £650 in gold for notes. Witness took him to the proper department to have exchange effected. On another occasion he brought £9,000 sovereigns of which *fifteen were light and those very slightly so.* [See my remarks in Chapter   about exchanging those sovereigns.—G. B.] On February 25th, he came again bringing 1,000 sovereigns. On that occasion the prisoner was kept waiting somewhat longer than usual, and was very fidgety. He rang the bell once or twice and wanted to know the reason of the detention. He had been detained half or three-quarters of an hour.

Mr. Joseph Reese Adams, principal of the issue department, said he recognized the prisoner, McDonald. He saw him on the 28th of January at the bank and asked him where he got the gold. The reply was either that it came from Lisbon, or that he brought it from Lisbon. Being asked if he got the gold from Knowles & Foster, of Lisbon, to whom the bank shipped largely, he said he did not. The weight of sovereigns was twenty-one pounds troy-weight to the 1,000.

At this point, the court having sat nearly seven hours, the case was adjourned until the following day at ten o'clock. The jury, as before, were conveyed in charge of the ushers of the court to the Terminus Hotel, Cannon Street.

It might become tedious to go into all the details of this memorable trial, in the course of which innumerable trifles—each unimportant by itself—were brought out during the examination of 108 witnesses from various parts of the world, until these became a web that enwrapped and rendered escape impossible.

I will, however, give some of the salient events of the trial, and hasten on to the final catastrophe, followed by the dramatic events during my fifteen years' incarceration.

The box was afterwards opened in the presence of witness, who found in it three bundles of bonds, representing in all $220,920. He also found in it some visiting cards bearing the name George Bidwell, two watches, some wearing apparel, and dies for stamping. Some of the bonds were wrapped in a nightshirt, and others in some soiled linen. The box was opened in the presence of several witnesses whom witness named. Witness eventually handed all the contents over to the receiver, who gave witness a receipt for them.

Mr. Charles M. Da Costa was next called. He deposed that he was a member of the law firm of Blatchford, Seward, Griswold & Da Costa, of New York, who he said had acted as solicitors there to the Bank of England during these proceedings. He was present at the opening of the trunk produced, and afterwards had delivered to him the bonds produced, and other property, by Mr. Jarvis, the receiver appointed by the Supreme Court of New York. The property having been claimed, as the direct proceeds of the forgeries, it was immediately turned over to Mr. Peter Williams, of the firm of Messrs. Freshfield, solicitors to the bank. It included American bonds worth in English money about £45,000, which were tightly folded up in three parcels, just as they were now, at the bottom of the trunk among some soiled linen. The trunk also contained some watches and dies, with the monogram " G. B." engraved on them, also a little bag of foreign coins, a large collection of shells, an elegant new dressing-gown, and clothes of different kinds. Witness also obtained from the post-office at New York, through Mr. Jarvis, the receiver, the two packages produced, one addressed G. C. Brownell, Esq., Brevoort House, Fifth Avenue, New York, and the other addressed Austin   Esq., New York, U. S. A., care of New York Safety Deposit Co., No. 140 Broadway. They had been detained there by Mr. Jarvis, the receiver in the suit, and handed over to witness's firm eventually. The envelope of the second letter bore English stamps, and the New York postmark of March 13, 1873. It was a registered letter, and bore the London postmark of the 25th of February last, and also the Cannon Street postmark. It contained bonds for $17,500 or $17,600, equivalent to about £3,700 in English money, and the seals on the envelopes corresponded with one of the dies found in the trunk. The other package, addressed G. C. Brownell, Esq., bore the New York postmark of March 20, 1873, and also contained $17,500. It likewise bore a similar seal to that of the other. Witness also procured from the receiver a letter (produced) addressed George M. McDonald, Esq., Post-office, New York City, U. S. A. It was dated the 11th of March last, and bore the Edinburgh postmark of that date, and that of New York of March 24th. It also bore part of the impression of a seal with the monogram " G. B." Witness also produced other letters similar in various respects, found in the trunk, and with that his evidence concluded.

Chapter XIX.

THE TRIAL CONTINUED—EIGHTH AND LAST DAY, TUESDAY, AUGUST 26TH—AN AFFECTING LETTER—NOYES TRIES TO SAVE THE OLD HOMESTEAD—HE LIKES TO STAY IN EUROPE!—A LETTER OF CONDOLENCE—MY LETTERS FROM EDINBURGH—THE CASE FOR THE PROSECUTION CLOSED—MR. METCALF, Q. C., TAKES A FORMAL OBJECTION, WHICH IS OVERRULED—MR. GIFFARD, Q. C., SUMS UP THE EVIDENCE ON THE PART OF THE PROSECUTION—McDONALD'S STATEMENT TO THE JURY—GEORGE BIDWELL'S REMARKS CUT SHORT BY JUDGE ARCHIBALD—MR. McINTIRE'S PLEA FOR AUSTIN —MR. RIBTON ADDRESSES THE JURY ON BEHALF OF NOYES—JUDGE ARCHIBALD SUMS UP—JURY RETIRES—BRING IN A VERDICT OF "GUILTY"—AUSTIN EXONERATES THE BANK MANAGER—LAST APPEAL OF THE PRISONERS—SENTENCED FOR LIFE.

THIS was the most interesting day in a trial of unprecedented interest. The court-room of the Old Bailey was packed, and, as on other occasions, the lobbies were filled and a crowd in the street waiting in the hope of eventually obtaining admission. Many of the nobility and gentry were present.

Mr. Giffard, Q. C., put in several letters written by the prisoners, and they were read by Mr. Read, the deputy clerk of arraigns. The first was written by Noyes to a brother in America, enclosing a letter of credit for £1,000 obtained by him on January 29th from Messrs. Baring Brothers:

LONDON, January 29, 1873.

DEAR BROTHER J——,—I have this day registered a letter to you containing £1,000 sterling, which you will collect to the best advantage. The bankers will charge from one-eighth to one-quarter per cent. for collection. There is a premium on London Exchange. Before collecting it post yourself as to exchange, so that they will not charge you exorbitant rates. On it you will get two premiums — that on London, and the difference between the value of gold and greenbacks. I think it will amount to about $5,500 ; I cannot tell exactly, but do the best you can. After you collect it carry $1,400 over to C―― to pay S――. $750; he will also pay that bond of $600 that father owes H―― K―― for that woodland. The bond is indorsed by J―― McL――, so you will see that K―― will sicken at the prospect of getting a hold of our homestead. The bond in Pratt Street let remain until my return. Take $250 yourself, to buy your wife a $150 sewing machine and other things as a present from me. Do not let anyone else know but that you bought them yourself. Also, deduct your expenses to go to Springfield and out home. Also, hand Robert C―― $50 if he should want it as a loan. Take a receipt for it, to be paid to father when convenient, if I am not at home. The balance you may place to my account in the First National Bank of Hartford, subject to be drawn by my sister in case of accident to me, or death, or a longer absence than six months. Make it draw interest. If they will not give interest, put it into the Ætna Bank. H―― will introduce you. I am trying to persuade a friend of mine, an English gentleman, to go to America and enter business. If I succeed it will perhaps throw us together. It is not certain when I shall return to America. These Englishmen are such sticklers for country it is hard to start them. I confess that I am beginning to like to stay in Europe. [Poor fellow! He is staying abroad longer than he likes.― G. B.] More anon. Yours ever, ED.

The following letters were written by George Bidwell shortly after his escape from Ireland, while in hiding at Edinburgh:

EDINBURGH, March 13, 1873.

DEAR M., — Your friend has had a series of the most extraordinary adventures since you saw him; a hell's chase, and no mistake. His nerve has stood him through two taps on shoulder and several encounters with detectives. He has been a Fenian, a priest, a professor, a Frenchman, a German, a Russian, who could speak only a "veree leetle Englese, mais un peu de Français et Allemand," and a deaf and dumb man with a slate and pencil — all in the space of a week.

March 18.

It made me nearly sick to read what I enclose. [Alluding to what I saw in the papers, showing how our real names had transpired, through my plans in the way of precautions not having been executed as I all along supposed.—G. B.] It is all right as long as I keep inland, but the moment I touch the borders there is the devil to pay. I ran through an awful gauntlet last week in Ireland. Who would have dreamed they could have got on track so soon as that! There was a job put up from Hastings, and I had a hard rub at Cx [meaning Charing Cross]. I am delaying, as every day changes my appearance. Of course it is impossible to say what move or when I shall make one, but my present opinion is that I shall be in London when this reaches you. The telegraph, and I suspect the post also, is an open book for these parties. I suppose they have procured special permit.' Therefore, do not on any account use the telegraph.

Mr. Albert Gearing, proprietor of the Terminus Hotel, London Bridge, who was called at the request of Mr. Ribton, proved that the prisoner, Austin   in the name of C. J. Horton, hired on the 11th of January last a sitting-room in his hotel, and that he subsequently introduced the prisoner Noyes as his clerk. The room was kept until February 21st.

That was the case for the prosecution. A formal objection was taken by Mr. Metcalf, Q. C., on the part of McDonald, that it had not been proved, in conformity with the Extradition Act, that the crime with which he was now charged was that for which his surrender was obtained in America, but it was overruled by the judge.

Mr. Giffard, Q. C., then summed up the evidence adduced on the part of the prosecution. He said he was entitled, under recent statute, to elicit from his learned friends on the other side, whether they intended to call witnesses or not, and they having informed him that they were not about to present any further evidence to the jury, it became his duty to close, with a few remarks, the case which he had presented to their decision. It was clear as a matter of law that if the particular bill which they were now discussing was forged and uttered in pursuance of a common design and scheme participated in by all the prisoners, all of them were equally guilty, though only one of them actually traced the signature

upon it. The question, therefore, for the jury was whether
all or any of the prisoners had participated in a design to forge
and utter that among a 'great many other bills. Although
the unity of design comprised, as he urged, the whole of the
prisoners, yet the evidence applicable to each was, however,
identical, for they were all tainted with the same guilty
design. A scheme of this character and magnitude was hap-
pily very rare, if not quite unknown, in this country; for it
was incredible that persons like the prisoners should have
sought to taint the whole currency of commerce in this country by a portentous crime of this nature. The bank authorities had been twitted for being so easily led into a net of that
kind, but let the jury consider what were the circumstances in
which Colonel Francis, the manager of the Western Branch,
was placed. His customer was a person who pretended to be
conducting large commercial transactions in this country and
all over the Continent, and his bills were of the highest possible character, and were discounted and paid with facility.
If there had been ever any genuine business transacted by
the prisoner, Austin   let him call witness to prove it;
but in the absence of such proof, he denounced that business
as one for the mere manufacture of forged bills, and a device
to dispose of proceeds. Genuine bills to the amount of between £8,000 and £9,000 were first of all discounted by the
Bank of England, and these bills, it had been proved, were
purchased on the Continent by one or other of the prisoners.
They not only established the credit of Warren at the bank,
but they served as the models for the forged bills which were
subsequently sent in. In the forged bill in question, the form
upon which it was written, and the various stamps on its surface, were purchased by George Bidwell. It was filled in and
signed by McDonald, and it bore the endorsement of Austin
     [Austin was out of England, and did not put on the
endorsement.— G. B.], to whose credit the amount of the
discount was placed. It was therefore shown in this one
instance alone that three of the prisoners had been concerned

in forging and uttering the bill. £65,000 (about $325,000) had been expended by Noyes in the purchase of American bonds, and £10,000 by McDonald, and the rest of the money had gone in other directions — the whole of it having first been withdrawn from the Western Branch, then paid into Horton's account at the Continental Bank, and subsequently changed from gold into notes, and *vice versa*. The examination of the witnesses had proved that Austin had left England about the 18th of January, but though absent he was nevertheless engaged in the fraud, for he was found purchasing bills on the Continent, which served as models for other forged bills. [No bills purchased by him after January 18th served as models for forged bills. I supposing him to be on his way home, made it necessary that his continued presence on the Continent should be concealed from me. It was his engagement which caused him to remain in Europe. — G. B.] As to George Bidwell, it was proved beyond question that he had procured various stamps and plates from five different engravers, and that all those stamps appeared on the whole of the forged acceptances, and that he had written from Birmingham the letters to Col. Francis enclosing bills, many of which bore his endorsement. McDonald had been also shown to have filled in the bill forms, and forged the names of the drawers and acceptors. Mr. Giffard then referred to the case of the prisoner Noyes, urging that, so far from being an innocent clerk, as was alleged, he was one of the most active participators in the fraud, and that, like the others, he shared in the proceeds. In conclusion, he advised the jury to receive with great caution any statement which the prisoners, or any one of them, might make as to the innocence or guilt of the rest, observing that it would not be under oath, and that the person making it would not be exposed to any cross-examination, and could not be interrogated by the court. [David Howell, our solicitor, informed the prosecution of the subject on which McDonald and myself were intending to address the court and jury, thus enabling Mr. Giffard to forestall and frustrate any effects our subsequent statement of facts might have had in favor of my brother and Noyes.—G. B.] He asked the jury to say by their verdict that all the prisoners had been engaged in one common design to commit a crime, the magnitude of which was almost unexampled in the history of this country.

Mr. Metcalf, Q. C., addressing the court, said he had attended very carefully to the whole case on the part of McDonald, together with the summing up for the prosecution, and he did not think it would be attended with any good effect for him to address the jury. More than that, McDonald himself desired to make a statement with the consent of the Bench. Mr. Besley made a similar announcement on the part of the prisoner George Bidwell. The prisoner George McDonald then proceeded to address the jury, and the whole audience listened with deep attention. He said:

The statement I have to make to you, gentlemen of the jury, was alluded to towards the end of Mr. Giffard's speech, and from what he said, I perceive he has been informed or conceived some idea himself as to what it was my intention to say. He tells you that any statement which I can make to you is not evidence, and can be received by you only with great caution. I do not attempt to deny that, but nevertheless, I think that my statement will be supported by the testimony which the prosecution has elicited, and that it will merit at least a very careful consideration at your hands. I can easily concede that it would be very difficult in my case to make any difference whatever, but as I believe that no person is in a position to give a more accurate or faithful account of this whole business than I am, I propose to show you, that in the case of one person at least, if I cannot show it by direct evidence, it is certainly worthy of considerable attention—I mean the very great probability of Austin entire innocence in the actual fraud. My only reason for making this statement is that the truth may be known in regard to him, for I am well aware that every word I am saying to you now cuts from under my feet any hope that I may have entertained for myself. It seems to be the idea of the prosecution — an idea which they have endeavored by every means in their power to bring you to believe — Mr. Justice Archibald, interposing said : " As I understand you to say that what you are now saying cuts away the ground of any defense from under your own feet, I can only allow you to address the court and jury on your own behalf, and not on behalf of any other person. I do not know to whom you are alluding, but each of the prisoners are represented by counsel, and if you propose to address the jury on behalf of any other person beside yourself, I cannot allow you."

McDonald: I have not the audacity, my lord, to appear as counsel for any other of the prisoners. What I intend to say, is simply a statement of facts.

The Judge: You can urge anything on your own behalf.

McDonald: It is on my own behalf, but it is perfectly impossible to make the statement I am about to make without referring to the others. I was saying that the idea of the prosecution, which they have endeavored to inforce on your conviction, is that the original intention with which Austin George Bidwell, and myself, came over to this country was to perpetrate this fraud on the Bank of England. I think if that idea could be entertained it would argue for us a knowledge and a prescience something more than men of ordinary ability and attainments could pretend to. It would suppose that we were perfectly acquainted with the mode of doing business in England, that we knew some person or other who had an account with the Bank of England, that we could by some well-devised plan get sufficiently into the confidence of that person to obtain from him an introduction to the Bank of England, and that all the other minor details, which have been so fully explained in the course of this investigation, would all work together for our benefit, would all turn out precisely as we desired, and that in fact, nothing at all would interfere to prevent the carrying out of the fraud. When we

CIRCUMSTANCES, AGAIN. 187

first came to England, it was certainly with no such intention. Mr. Green, of Saville Row, has told you that the opening of the account with the Western Branch of the Bank of England was an entire accident, and so it was. That was done on May 4th, and on May 28th we three left England. We left England without the slightest intention of returning. Circumstances occurred to induce us to change our plans, and we came back two months later. There is no doubt but that the intention was to close the account with the Bank of England, because it was of no use. But when we came back to England it was of considerable use and advantage to us to cash any bills that might come to us.

We went from England to the Continent, and our intention, while there, was to do certain business between Vienna and Frankfort-on-the-Main. Circumstances arose while we were at Vienna to prevent that business. In the meantime I was taken very seriously ill, and returned to England for the benefit of medical advice. George Bidwell was in Amsterdam, and he sent me a bill drawn on Baring Bros., which I got cashed myself, by which I saw that the manner of doing business was entirely different than in America.

As soon as I saw how business was transacted, I sent a telegram from the station next adjoining the Alexandria Hotel, to George Bidwell, in Amsterdam, and I stated in that telegram that I had made a great discovery. That telegram, I dare say, could be found, but as it would tend to show that the fraud could not have been contemplated so early in the transaction, it has not been brought forward. In America, when bills are presented at a bank for discount, or when acceptances are presented, it is the custom to send them round to the persons accepting, to be what is technically called "initialed," in order that their validity and genuineness may be certified. I found that was not the case here, and the result of the discovery is, that I am standing before you to-day.

Mr. Pinto, from Amsterdam, has told you that George

Bidwell purchased bills drawn from Amsterdam upon Hamburg, which bills a day or two afterwards were sold again, and others drawn upon London purchased with the proceeds, and the bills so obtained were afterwards discounted by F. A. Warren. The matter went on in that way for some time, until the 11th or 12th of January Austin went over to Paris to buy the bill on Messrs. Rothschild which has been so much commented upon — that for £4,500. During this voyage or journey to Paris, he met with a very severe railroad accident, in which one man certainly was killed outright, and I think two or three more, and Austin had probably as narrow an escape from being smashed to pieces as any man ever did. On arriving in London he was in such a condition that it was almost impossible for him to move. He was taken to a hotel and visited by a physician, Doctor Coulson, who told him he was in very great danger of being paralyzed for life. On January 17th, when Austin took that bill to the bank, I went with him as far as the door, and afterwards helped him back to my quarters. I think on the following day the doctor saw him, and Austin then told him it was his intention to leave England immediately. The doctor informed him that if he intended to travel he must do so at once. The evidence goes to show that up to this time every preparation had been made for the contemplated fraud. January 18th was Saturday, and after the doctor's interview with Austin who was then in my room, he told me that it was his intention to utterly withdraw from anything connected with this or any other similar matter. You can easily conceive that up to this time a great deal of money had been thrown away in continually transferring the papers. The idea of losing that money and having no return for it was very displeasing, but as Austin was determined to leave, and did, I could only let him go. On Dr. Coulson's advice, Austin decided to travel at once, and he left with me two checks, one drawn on the Western Branch of the Bank of England, and the other on

Harcourts & Co. (Continental Bank), to obtain the balance of this account and invest the proceeds in United States bonds, which were to be forwarded to him in Paris. These two checks were cashed, and the proceeds left in my hands. The first forged bill was sent from Birmingham on January 21st. Mr. Chabot has told you that in his opinion the endorsement "F. A. Warren" on the bills was in his own handwriting. It was not. No one knows that better than I do. My hand was the one that put the endorsements on the forged bills of exchange.

Mr. Chabot, the expert, also says the checks on which the moneys were drawn from the two banks were in Austin   handwriting, and were all signed at one sitting. Several of them were signed at one sitting — I give that credit to Mr. Chabot — but not by Austin   I can refer you in particular to the check which went to the Western Branch of the Bank of England, in which the name of Horton was misspelled. It is admitted that Austin   was then on the way to Havana. Mr. Chabot does not state positively that these checks were signed by Horton; the Continental Bank was perfectly well satisfied that they were signed by Horton, and I think the expert in that bank was quite as well able to judge as Mr. Chabot whether the signatures were genuine.

Referring again to the accident on the Northern Railway of France — when Austin   arrived at my quarters in London, his first statement to me was this: "Mac, I have had as miraculous an escape from instant death as perhaps any man has ever experienced." He went on to elaborate his sentiments during the accident, and wound up by saying that so deep an impression had been made on his mind, in those few moments of peril, that he should certainly have nothing more to do with whatever might affect his personal convenience, liberty, and happiness in this world, but also place in jeopardy — according to the view from which he looked at it — his eternal happiness. I think, gentlemen of the jury, that this is not a far-fetched statement, but is probably one that will commend itself to your attention as being worthy of a great deal of consideration, namely, that a man of his age could not have so absolutely and entirely forgotten the sentiments implanted in youth as to be indifferent to such a warning. For myself I am willing to confess that, probably from not having gone through such an ordeal myself, I gave the matter but little attention for the moment; in fact, I laughed at it and at him; but all I could say did not change his mind, and on the following morning he left England.

He left everything in confusion, as far as this business is concerned, and in a state of unreadiness. When the first bills were sent into the bank, the intention only was to recoup the loss on the money transactions, and then clear out. But when the facility with which they were received and discounted was considered, it was determined to carry the thing farther, and to do so it was necessary to get up bills, have printing done, and stamps made, and there was very little time to do it in. Mr. Giffard, in his address, asked what was the object of the account. The object was very plain. I do not propose to insult your understandings, gentlemen, by saying that a fraud was not contemplated at one time, but you may perhaps be inclined to believe that such a statement as I am now making is made only with one motive. Does it redound to my advantage? does it help to clear me at all? or do I state to you anything that is intrinsically improbable? I think not. I have no doubt Mr. Giffard has had a great deal of experience in this sort of business, and I dare say he will believe me when I say men engaged in an illegitimate transaction do not place very much confidence in each other. And if there were an intention, in spite of the withdrawal of one party, still to carry out the original scheme, it is not likely that party, after having entirely withdrawn, should be intrusted with any confidence concerning the scheme. He asks who were benefited by it; and if he sifts the matter, I think it could be very easily explained. He said it would be very difficult to prove any such statement as I am now making, which is but the simple truth.

Since Mr. Chabot first took upon himself the profession of an expert, business of this kind, like every other, has made very great strides. It has become, as one of the newspapers said, an art.

The Judge: What business do you mean?

I mean fraud, and a very wretched, unhappy, miserable, and contemptible art — it may be to a certain extent called an art, nevertheless. Mr. Chabot would induce you to believe that these checks were left signed by Austin   I am unwilling to allow that statement to be left as it was by Mr. Chabot on your minds, when you come to meditate on your verdict. My only object is to make as much reparation as can be done to Austin   who, in spite of Mr. Giffard's statement as to its improbability, has been deceived and imposed upon, and has had his confidence violated. If I am successful in pressing that view of the case upon you, I shall have obtained all I can ask for. If I am not I can only regret it, but I ask when you go to consider your verdict, to bear in mind the statement I have made, to consider whether there is anything intrinsically improbable in it, and to say whether it is at all likely that I would stand up here and through any other motive than the one I have mentioned, make observations which must necessarily be prejudicial to myself. That is all, gentlemen, I have to say to you.

[Although I sat by McDonald's side when he made the above statement, I had forgotten what he said about the date of the first conception of the fraud and the opening of the Warren account at the Bank of England. What I have said in relation to those events in Chapter   and elsewhere, was written before I had seen his statement in print. It will be seen that our accounts agree. — G. B.]

The prisoner, George Bidwell, addressing the jury, said there was much he could have urged in his defense by way of comment on the evidence; but, nothwithstanding that, feeling from his sense of guilt in having aided in carrying out the forgeries, it had been his intention to throw himself on the mercy of the court. With that view he had prepared a statement; but after what Mr. McDonald had said, it would be mere repetition in him to attempt it. He confirmed that statement, which he said was the truth and nothing but the truth, adding that Noyes was never trusted by them, and only did what he was told to do. Mr. Justice Archibald, interposing, told the prisoner, George Bidwell, he must confine himself to his own defense, seeing that Noyes was defended by counsel. George Bidwell said he only wished to lay the facts before the court. Mr. Justice Archibald said he could have pleaded guilty, in which case he might have been called as a witness and given his evidence on oath. George Bidwell replied that he had not been aware of that. Mr. Justice Archibald said he might have been informed of it.

Mr. McIntyre, Q. C., speaking in behalf of Austin said he had to contend that the prosecution had failed to substantiate the charge preferred against his client. He knew perfectly well that the magnitude of a crime or the seriousness of the consequences of a verdict of guilty would never deter an English jury from doing their duty; but he was also sure that they would require in a case of that kind the clearest and most indisputable evidence, and failing to obtain it, however suspicious the surrounding circumstances might be, they would acquit the prisoner. He urged that the evidence was utterly inconsistent with the guilt of Austin

A great mass of evidence had been placed before them, showing the antecedent connection of the prisoners, and a vast number of other circumstances, but he challenged them to find any proof that, with the bill in question, Austin forged or uttered it, or was even aware of the forgery. They could not convict him unless they actually believed that he was concerned in the fabrication of the bill, or that it was carried out with his cognizance and connivance. It had been clearly proved that some time in 1872 the brothers Bidwell and McDonald were living in an obscure neighborhood in London, and that on paying a casual visit to Mr. Green, their tailor, in Saville Row, Austin producing a large sum of money requested him to take it and keep it until his return from a short journey. Mr. Green hesitated, and upon his suggestion he introduced the prisoner, unfortunately for him, to the authorities at the Western Branch, who at once agreed to open an account with him. He contended that at that moment there was no fraudulent design upon the bank, and that to the end of the year, and even for some time in January the transactions in respect to that account were perfectly honest.

The prisoner left this country on January 18th, three days before the first batch of forged bills arrived from Birmingham, and from that time his personal connection with the account ceased. Mr. McIntyre complained that the bank authorities had not thought fit to make any inquiries at the address which the prisoner gave in London, and that although possessing a branch at Birmingham they never instituted any investigation as to the solvency or to the position of their customer, who represented himself to be living there and from whom they were receiving almost daily large batches of bills.

It is also inconceivable that they should without suspicion have dealt so largely with a person who only gave his address at the post-office in that town. The prosecution had failed to prove that Austin was ever at Birmingham in his life. It had been admitted by Col. Francis that he at first believed all the letters containing the bills to be in Warren's handwriting, and the bills to bear his indorsement, but it has since been proved by Mr. Chabot that nearly all those letters and indorsements were written by George and not by Austin He urged that such was the case in the bill in question, and he asked the jury to believe that Austin had never seen either of them, he being out of England at the time. It was quite clear that Austin possessed money of his own, for before any of the forged bills were discounted, £17,000 had passed through the bank in respect of his account. It was thus that he accounted for the possession of the bonds and money found at Havana, and for the circumstances that his brother and McDonald sent him other bonds on his journey thither. It might be that he was willing to join in the venture to some extent, but it was clear that after his accident he changed his mind and had nothing more to do with the matter. All the stamps and blocks were purchased after he left, and not one of the forged bills was presented while he was in the country. In conclusion Mr. McIntyre made an earnest appeal to the jury to acquit his client.

Mr. Ribton followed on behalf of Noyes, observing that his case differed entirely from that of any other, and that there was not a tittle of evidence which would warrant the jury in convicting him. On December 17th Noyes arrived in Liverpool from America and went to London, where he inserted an advertisement in a newspaper applying for a situation as a clerk or partner. The result was that he was taken into the service of the prisoner, Austin who had assumed the name of Horton, and he deposited with him as security the sum of £300. A formal agreement was entered into on January 11th between the parties, and on the same day Horton took an office at the London Bridge Hotel, and introduced Noyes as his clerk. From that time to the date of his arrest he discharged the duties of his position, and these duties had special reference to the paying in or cashing of checks on his master's account at the Continental Bank, and the purchase of American securities.

The jury would recollect that the fraud of the other prisoners commenced in May last, when the account at the Bank of England was opened — that between May and November they were engaged upon the Continent, in purchasing genuine bills as models, and that the account of Horton at the Continental Bank commenced on the 2d of December. All these transactions happened, therefore, before Noyes arrived in

England, and he had no knowledge of them. He was evidently acquainted with the other prisoners, as it was proved that he associated with them directly upon his arrival in London, but he was entirely ignorant of any fraud that was in contemplation, and so he remained down to the time of his arrest. Not a single fact has been proved which would lead to the belief that he was concerned in the forgery, but throughout the whole transaction he had been the innocent dupe of the other men. He admitted that his client had assumed other names than his own but none of them had been used to promote the fraudulent scheme. There was no evidence to show that Noyes had any knowledge of Warren's account at the Western Branch or that he ever saw any of the forged bills, and there was good ground for believing he was kept in darkness on all these points. The jury might regard him if they chose as an adventurer who was anxious to make money, but there was not a scintilla of evidence to show that he had ever been connected with the forgery. It was perfectly clear that Noyes had been selected to perform the part of an innocent assistant.

Mr. Justice Archibald in summing up said the prisoners were indicted for forging and uttering a bill of exchange for £1,000 with intent to defraud. That was the offense charged against them, but in the course taken by the prosecution they had laid before the jury evidence to show that the prisoners were all concerned in a fraudulent scheme for the purpose of defrauding the Bank of England. He did not propose to minutely go over the evidence adduced in the case, because it would doubtless be fresh in the minds of the jury, and especially after the statements of the prisoners George Bidwell and McDonald who had virtually admitted their guilt. McDonald had openly confessed his participation in the fraud, and George Bidwell had adopted his statement though without confessing his guilt. As regards George Bidwell, there was no doubt that he was guilty of forging the bill in question and many others. The learned judge then reviewed the evidence with great care, with a view to ascertain for the guidance of the jury how far the remaining prisoners Austin and H had been concerned in the fraud. He observed that Austin had left England in January, yet if he made arrangements for the forgery to be continued in his name he was just as guilty as though he had written and signed the bill himself.

The jury retired to consider their verdict shortly after seven o'clock, and on returning into court after the lapse of about quarter of an hour, they gave in a verdict of guilty against all of the four prisoners.

On being asked if they had anything to say why sentence should not be passed upon them, Austin replied that he had nothing to say for himself, but that he would take advantage of the only opportunity he would have to repair a wrong he had done to a gentleman then in court, and for which he was extremely sorry. He alluded to Col. Francis, manager of the Western Branch, hoping that as years rolled on he would forget the wrong. That gentleman had been the subject of considerable criticism, but speaking from his knowledge of the case, he would say any other man in London would have been deceived in the same manner.

George McDonald observed that he had nothing to say of the verdict as far as he was concerned, but that Noyes was ignorant of the forgery, and Austin at the time out of England.

George Bidwell said he did not ask any consideration for himself, but he begged that his brother, who was a young man and but recently married, might be dealt with mercifully. Referring to the prisoner Noyes, he said that he had been kept in ignorance of the real state of the affairs.

Noyes, addressing the court, said he was innocent of the proceedings of the other prisoners, and was kept in the dark as to who the man Warren was. He concluded by making an earnest appeal to the judge to temper justice with mercy.

Judge Archibald proceeded to pass sentence. He said: If I could conceive a worse case of forgery, then less than the maximum might have been sufficient; but, *as I cannot conceive a worse case*,* I cannot perceive a reason for mitigating the sentence. That sentence is, that each and all of you be kept in penal servitude for life, and, in addition to that, I order that each of you shall pay one quarter of the costs of the prosecution [£35,000].

---

* Justice Archibald "cannot conceive a worse case" of forgery! After our crime has been expiated by fifteen years of the worst kind of slavery — while not wishing to palliate anything in the way of crime, or even anything that violates the *Cardinal Principle of life*, "treating others as we should wish to be treated"— I can do no less than call attention to the apparent prejudice against us exhibited by him on numerous occasions during the trial. And this is well illustrated by the preceding paragraph. If the honorable Judge is still alive, let him answer the following question: Considered in its moral bearings, and, judging from the relative degree of misery caused, which is the worst act : To obtain money by fraud from a corporation like the Bank of England, to which millions are but a drop in the bucket, or to get away the investments and savings of thousands, including the jointures of widows and the inheritances of orphans, leaving them to drag out lives amid deprivation and want — and worse? To give but one of dozens of instances which have happened in this very England during our imprisonment: The managers of the Glasgow Bank perpetrated all the enormities shadowed forth above. . The evidence was conclusive, and the proofs indisputable, but they were not Americans, had influential friends, and therefore got off with sentences varying from twelve months to two years. They were soon again at liberty to perpetrate fresh frauds, leaving those of their victims who are not dead to struggle to this day for existence — some of their fair daughters to end wretched lives as *nymphs du pavé*, and I have seen some of the sons in prison.—G. B.

The son of the judge who tried us at the Old Bailey, Mr. Archibald, now a barrister of the Temple, London, states: "During the trial I sat beside my father, taking notes for him. Hundreds of Americans flocked to the court. The scene on the last day was extraordinary. Every one believed a rescue would be attempted. That is why you were sentenced without a moment's delay after the jury had rendered the verdict of 'guilty.' Besides the swarms of officers in uniform and in citizen's dress, all officials, including the judge and officers of the court, were armed; and we all breathed a sigh of relief when the sentence of 'penal servitude for life' was passed and you four Americans were safe behind the bars of Newgate. Were my father now alive and had the sentence to pronounce again, I do not believe it would be one of life for your brother and Noyes. I have no doubt, if alive, he would sign a petition for their release, which I am glad to do, and will aid your efforts for the release of your brother Austin to the best of my ability."

Good-natured reader — you who have followed my tortuous footsteps almost through a lifetime — a lifetime of experiences the like of which I trust may never fall to the lot of another — the limit of this volume is now reached — the end has come!

The months occupied in the preparation of these pages have been — aside from painful but necessary retrospections — a period of unalloyed happiness. Freedom — home — friends! — why should I not be happy? Instead of the coldness and rebuffs, which the unwarranted proceeding in New York harbor led me to anticipate, I have received only kindness, encouragement, and valued assistance from the best men and women in the world. Fortunate indeed it is that my associations and surroundings have been of so healthful a character. Would that all, in circumstances corresponding with my own, might enjoy like ennobling influences!

What more fitting time than this beautiful day in June for paying my tribute of acknowledgment to those benefactors? Reclining dreamily, my attention is aroused by the hum of bees around my hammock, which swings from the friendly projecting arms of a conical-shaped pine at the foot of the lawn, its myriads of tufts and buds swaying to the summer breeze and filling the air with soft murmurs. Glancing upward, my view is obstructed by majestic ancestral elms, together forming a gigantic bower. The melody among the grand old boughs reveals the nesting-places of many birds. Joyous creatures! Who would not be happy as a bird in June? Alas! my lost — irrevocably lost — scores of Junes! How full of life everything appears. Yonder a squirrel scurries circling up the trunk of a poplar. Apple, quince, cherry, and plum trees,

> With flowers and shrubs, here widely spread,
> Shed rich perfumes around my head.

A pair of robin red-breasts are hopping fearlessly about; there to the left, a little jenny-wren is picking at the pea-blossoms, the product of seed planted and tended by my own hands, from which I hope ere long to be rewarded by a feast of green peas — the first in fifteen years! It is too pleasant, the air too delicious, to remain indoors; and seated near me is the modern Penelope — from whom Folly separated me so long — watching the sports of grandchildren. Their merry laughter brings to the youthful-appearing grandmother's lips an answering smile, and a look of the old-time happiness to her still handsome features.

Somehow, I feel that when these closing words of mine are being read, I shall be permitted to regard each reader as a *friend*. To such I say in parting, Come and see me at my pleasant home amid the elms — wife, children, grandchildren, clustering around me. John Howard Payne could never have appreciated "Home, Sweet Home" as I now do.

Good-bye, dear readers — and in the language of Tiny Tim, "God bless us every one!"

G. B

"*The Elms,*" *East Hartford, Conn.*

APPENDIX.

AUSTIN CASE.

AFTER eighteen years' incarceration on a life sentence at twenty-five, charged with a crime against property only, viz.: being an accomplice in the passing of fraudulent bills of exchange on the Bank of England, for which he has been punished beyond all reason, and that opinion is sustained by the officials of the bank, who have written to the American minister that they will not oppose his release, he says :

, "Counting from my birth to this hour, I have passed more than one-third of an ordinary lifetime in a Chatham prison cell. If we exclude the immaturity of youth and the helplessness of old age, then I have lost more than one-half of my earthly life. And is there any crime under heaven where property alone is involved that such an ETERNITY OF SUFFERING ought not to expiate? I do not intend to say anything more on that point, either now or at a future time; I only desire to remark that if I am rescued at all, it must be soon. But if left to perish in my misery, I will not repine."

The following is an extract from a late letter:

"Truly, if a man in my position means not to be conquered, he must laugh at all physical discomfort, however severe. Still, I have not yet attained such perfection of character as to enable me to enjoy suffering, nor am I so in love with the extreme of misery and wretchedness as to want it to continue one hour longer than is absolutely necessary. I really think it time that my transgressions might be forgiven and forgotten. My early manhood and all my prime have gone to pay the debt, and still more is required. But let them pour on, *I will endure*, don't fear for that."

NOTE.— After serving nineteen years from date of his arrest the writer of above letters was reprieved, since this Appendix was published in pamphlet form. Efforts will not cease until the other two Americans shall be freed — all four having been adjudged equally guilty.

200   *APPENDIX.*

A PARODY ON JUSTICE.

Atrocious murderers have been pardoned out of this same Chatham prison during the time Austin has been incarcerated there. Here are the names of five only:

Charles Wales, sentenced to death in 1874, but changed to penal servitude for life. Released in 1884.

McConnion, a soldier, sentenced to death in 1877 because he kicked his victim to death, was an out-and-out ruffian and a bad character in prison. At time of commutation of sentence the Home Secretary said that the only ground for commutation to penal servitude for life was because the military authorities erred in not removing the boots from his feet when put in the guard-house. He was released in 1887 simply because his colonel desired it.

George Ash, sentenced at Stafford in 1874 for cutting his wife's throat (not quite fatally); two previous convictions for assaulting her. Twenty years' sentence and a free pardon in 1884.

Wood, sentenced for a similar offense to life, in 1879, pardoned in August, 1889.

Lascelle, a Manchester banker, for shooting his wife, sentenced in 1881 for 20 years, and pardoned in August, 1889.

Mr. Hind Smith, of the Y. M. C. A., Exeter Hall, London, and E. J. Bassett, Esq., of the Ætna Insurance Company, Hartford, Conn., and others, went to Chatham prison to visit Austin They were greatly pleased with the interview, and said that the authorities spoke of him in the highest terms, and declared that he was the best man ever under their charge.

In 1886, after he had been incarcerated thirteen years, the Home Secretary replied to a petition for his release: "That it was too early as yet to entertain the question." Many years have since passed, and he still languishes in Chatham prison.

In 1873 Sir Sidney Waterlow examined 108 witnesses against the accused; therefore he was able to judge as to the varying degrees of their guilt. After an interval of seventeen years the writer met him in the fall of 1890 at the Windsor hotel, New York. Almost his first words were: "George Bidwell, your brother ought to have been freed years ago, and you kept." I have proved there was no mistake in freeing me; why hold the lesser guilty?

"Lord Hershell brought before the House of Lords the subject of the inequality of sentences. Mr. Justice Matthews has recently protested with righteous indignation against the monstrous penalties imposed by some judges for petty acts of theft. Lord (Judge) Coleridge has repeatedly uttered such remonstrances. Some of her Majesty's judges deal out periods of penal servitude with positively frightful recklessness. It is almost

To show the opinions of some of England's greatest men, I have the honor to submit copies of letters, etc., appended to a petition for Austin   release. Notwithstanding the influence of such eminent names, the petition was refused, because of what was said by the American press about my own release — some of the newspapers asserting that I would unfailingly plunge back into crime. Of course, if that should prove to be the truth, the authorities would be justified in preventing him from joining me in a criminal career. But I trust the time is not distant when they will be disabused of that belief.

JOHN BRIGHT.

18 Clifford Street, W. (London).

DEAR MR. MATTHEWS, — May I venture to ask you to consider the case to which this letter or memorial refers, and to express my opinion that to consent to the petition would be an act not only of mercy but of wisdom.

A life sentence on a young man of 25 years of age for an offense against property, seems to me very harsh and inconsistent with the better feeling prevailing in our time.

Pray forgive me for thus addressing you. An act of mercy will not lessen the confidence of the public in your eminent office.

Yours very sincerely,

JOHN BRIGHT.

---

always, however, for offenses against property that these ferocious punishments are inflicted. It is a sad commentary on the so-called Christian civilization of England that the administration of its laws should often give more protection to the property of the rich than to the lives of the poor."— *London paper.*

To Right Hon. H. MATTHEWS, *Home Office:*

July 12, 1887.

I heartily support the request of Mr. Bright.

J. CHAMBERLAIN (M. P.).

Aug. 1, 1887.

It does appear as if a life sentence at 25 was as severe as could have been had the case been the worst possible to men.

Surely a careful revision is not too much to ask. I earnestly join my request to that of Mr. Bright.

(The Reverend) CHARLES H. SPURGEON.

Aug. 4, 1887.

I agree with the above.

RANDOLPH T. CHURCHILL (M. P.).

I strongly support Mr. Bright's request.

JOHN MORLEY (M. P.).

I heartily support Mr. Bright's request.

(The Marquis of) LYMINGTON.

I hope the case will be reconsidered.

(The Marquis of) HARTINGTON.

Aug. 6, 1887.

I think there is here a very strong case for the consideration of the Home Secretary.

CHARLES RUSSELL (Queen's Coun.).

George Bidwell has made a record since his release, which has won him the support of the best people, as is attested by numerous letters in his possession, also by the following selections from many notices of his efforts on the platform. The British government made no mistake in freeing him and need not fear to place his brother under his influence.

[From the Worcester *Spy*, Worcester, Mass., Feb. 28, 1890.]

Society is none the worse because George Bidwell is again at large. On the contrary, no one could listen to the pathetic and unvarnished story as told by him last night at Horticultural

Hall, without feeling that society has been the gainer by his liberation, and that many young men who may perhaps be on the brink of taking such a fatal plunge as he took may be warned in time.

[Boston Daily *Globe* of Wednesday, March 11, 1890.]

A large audience gathered in Tremont Temple last evening, to listen to George Bidwell's lecture on "Forging His Chains." It was probably one of the most thrilling and impressive lectures ever delivered before a Boston audience, and was fully illustrated by stereopticon colored views, descriptive of American and English prisons, also views of the uniforms worn by the prison wardens, guards, and convicts. A pathetic letter written by his brother, now incarcerated in an English prison where he has already served eighteen years of his life, was produced on the screen.

[Boston *Herald* of Wednesday, March 11, 1890.]

A man who spent over fourteen years in English prisons told something about them to an audience in Tremont Temple last night. It was George Bidwell, the now famous author of "Forging His Chains," who, in 1873, was sentenced to penal servitude for life for frauds on the Bank of England, and was released three or four years ago on ticket of leave.

All his efforts on the lecture platform and in the field of authorship are now devoted to securing means with which to prosecute his endeavors in behalf of his younger brother Austin, who was sentenced with him eighteen years ago, and is still in prison in England.

Mr. Bidwell made a good appearance on the stage. His earnest words went straight to the hearts of his hearers, and were rewarded with frequent applause. The "entertainment," as he called it, consisted of a brief sketch of his early life, the exhibition and explanation of a series of stereopticon views of prison scenes and kindred matters, and an account of his pursual and capture by detectives in 1873.

The lecture was full of sound moral precepts and devoid of sensational claptrap. "I am confident," Mr. Bidwell said, "that without exception, the men who take the money of others and give nothing in return inevitably come to misery and degradation." In another place he spoke of the self-justification of roguery in which hardened rascals always indulge. "They are led on from step to step," he said, "until dishonesty becomes their second nature, and **they** believe it is right."

Speaking of the customary solitary confinement of nine months at the beginning of a term in an English prison, he declared that it was put on at the wrong end of the term. He referred in complimentary words to the prison vans in use in England, and, on the other hand, called the prison vans of the United States "a disgrace to civilization," in which sentiment the audience seemed to agree with him.

The last picture shown was that of his faithful wife, who preserved his home for him during all those long years of his imprisonment. She was in the audience. In response to the applause that greeted the exhibition of her picture, he said: "In behalf of that noble wife who is present at my lecture to-night for the first time, I thank you for your generous approval."

In relating the incidents of his flight and capture, Mr. Bidwell became very much animated and made use of some vigorous expressions. "I took to being hunted naturally," he said, "although that was the first time I was ever pursued by officers."

The last thing on the programme, and perhaps the most striking feature of all, was his appearance in English prison costume. While thus dressed, he recited "The Captive's Prayer" and "The Prisoner's Dream," verses composed by him in prison. This formed a thrilling climax to a thoroughly interesting lecture.

[Special to the New York *World* of December 28, 1890.]

HARTFORD, Dec. 27, 1890.

Of all the men who walk the streets of Hartford not one has a life history more eventful than has George Bidwell, who was liberated by the English Government a few years ago. He walks the streets as a free man, equal in all things to any freeman on God's footstool. That he is leading an honest and sacrificing life is doubted by no one who knows him.

Mr. Bidwell lives with his family in a cosy cottage on the east side of the river. His wife remained true to him, and after many years they were again united. He is now a man of nearly sixty years, somewhat bent and quite lame, the result of his imprisonment in England.

In his canvassing tours, which have extended from Maine to the far West, he has usually met with a cordial reception. He relates some instances, however, which greatly amused him at the time and of which he speaks when drawn out. On one occasion he entered a bank, approached the cashier and introduced himself, adding that he was taking subscriptions for "Forging His Chains." The cashier did not throw up his hands in holy horror, but he did the next thing possible — he was seized with the shivers. He curtly replied that he did not wish the book. Politely bowing, Mr. Bidwell started for the door bearing the words "President's Office."

The cashier went crazy, and, springing from his stool, he rushed out of his wire cage and grabbed the lame book agent by the collar.

"You cannot see the President!" shouted the cashier in a voice loud enough to be heard all over the room, and added still louder, "A forger in the bank! Get out quick."

Mr. Bidwell left, but feels certain to this day that that cashier had been engaged in fraud of some kind, to be so sensitive and at the same time so pure. For a long time he watched the papers, expecting a defalcation in the bank.

Among other places where he got snubbed and was considered unclean was in the People's Savings Bank at Worcester. The treasurer subscribed for a copy of the book, when he approached Teller Kimball, the latter having a fit of the horrors. The bank official was afraid of pollution, and waved the book agent away with a nickel-plated wave — one of the graceful species acquired only after weeks of patient practice — one of those far-away, searching, "git-out-of-this" kind. Mr. Bidwell suspected the man, and in a week or more Kimball and the bank's money were among the missing.

Another guilty man who cared not to read "Forging His Chains," was Robinson, the Brockton (Mass.) forger. This alleged sample of piety held his head high on the occasion of Mr. Bidwell's visit, and a day or two later was enjoying the atmosphere of Canada.

But the bank men take kindly to the one of all others who was held in the greatest fear. He has been entertained by some of the leading bankers of New York, Chicago, and other cities, and feelingly refers to the confidence of these men in him.

Mr. Bidwell has also distinguished himself as a lecturer.

Under the encouragement of prominent persons it had been my intention to go to England to lecture, in the hope of affecting a revulsion of feeling in favor of my imprisoned friends, but the following threat has caused me to give up the idea for the present:

"With reference to Mr. George Bidwell's letter of the 17th November, stating that it is his desire to return to England for the purpose of giving lectures, and enquiring as to the conditions under which the revocation of his License could be enforced, the Under Secretary of State has to inform him that his License is revocable at pleasure, and that no encouragement can be held out to him to return to England for the purpose mentioned. If Mr. George Bidwill does so return, it must be entirely at his own risk.

WHITEHALL, 7th January, 1891."

I have letters from merchants and clergymen — competent judges — that my public lectures are having a most salutary effect in keeping young men from giving way to the countless temptations which *their parents* as members of Society *permit* to surround and engulf them unawares. These are far worse than twenty years since. By all means keep me out of England!

This spring of 1891 makes nearly four years since my liberation. The past three of these I have been before the public, and have made a record which has won me the support of the best people.

After losing fifteen years of my prime, and in view of above record, is it not very hard to cause me to continue expending all the earnings gained by the severest labor of sixteen hours a day with feet, pen, and tongue, for the sale of my book, in the work to obtain the liberation of my brother, who has been punished beyond all reason? And this does not take into account the fact that in earning this money I have been obliged to be away from my wife, children, and grandchildren — absent from that pleasant home in East Hartford. If the British Government are dissatisfied with the amount of my punishment, as *partially* detailed in "Forging His Own Chains," then I will put myself in their hands again. It looks as though they hold my brother and punish me now, as above, out of vexation and spite at, in their view, the serious mistake of ever having freed me. But the Bidwells have pluck, and will never cease until Austin Bidwell shall be freed.

www.ingramcontent.com/pod-product-compliance
Lightning Source LLC
Chambersburg PA
CBHW031819220426
43662CB00007B/715